GO THE DISTANCE

The inspirational story of Tom Tunison,
Thurman Munson and a lifelong quest for baseball immortality.

TOM TUNISON

with

GARY KASCHAK

Black Rose Writing | Texas

©2022 by Tom Tunison
All rights reserved. No part of this book may be reproduced, stored in a retrieval system or transmitted in any form or by any means without the prior written permission of the publishers, except by a reviewer who may quote brief passages in a review to be printed in a newspaper, magazine or journal.

The author grants the final approval for this literary material.

First printing

ISBN: 978-1-68513-030-5
PUBLISHED BY BLACK ROSE WRITING
www.blackrosewriting.com

Printed in the United States of America
Suggested Retail Price (SRP) $20.95

Go the Distance is printed in EB Garamond

*As a planet-friendly publisher, Black Rose Writing does its best to eliminate unnecessary waste to reduce paper usage and energy costs, while never compromising the reading experience. As a result, the final word count vs. page count may not meet common expectations.

Edited by James Beemer

To Suzette
My beautiful wife and best friend
I love you

To Diana Munson
Thank you for "Going the Distance" with Thurman all these years and for all of the amazing work you have done in his name with AHRC and for loving his fans... we love you

To Mom and Dad and Larry and Brenda
I wouldn't be here without your amazing love and support... I am eternally grateful

To my three God-fearing sons, Thomas, Daniel and James and their beautiful wives, Courtney, Michelle and Kelly:
Trust in Him always: John 3:16

And to my God in Heaven
All the Glory... all of it

GO THE DISTANCE

Foreword
By Dwier Brown

To say that my role as John Kinsella in the movie Field of Dreams changed my life would be an understatement. Of all of the hundred parts I played onscreen and onstage, nothing compares with the five minutes of screen time I had in that film. (for exposure, fan-building, emotional bonding and, yes, magical experiences).

My tiny scene with Kevin Costner has been included in the American Film Institute's Top 100 Movie Scenes of All Time, it is perennially on the top of lists of the Best Sports Movies and was recently enshrined in the National Film Registry of the Library of Congress.

But what has been more gratifying by far has been my profound interactions with fans over the years. Strangers who have told me about the deep impact the film has had on them, the sense of hopefulness and joy it has brought them over the years and the changes it has motivated in their relationships, particularly with fathers and sons and daughters.

I have heard tearful confessions about careers changed, businesses birthed and countless dreams pursued (many of them selfless and philanthropic)—all because of the inspiration provided by this magical movie.

So it was no great surprise when, while selling my book If You Build It... at a baseball card show in Batavia, New York, I was enthusiastically approached by a handsome, middle-aged man who seemed to be fluttering between tears and laughter at the unexpected sight of John Kinsella standing in front of him on a rainy day in Upstate New York.

After a long discussion of the serendipitous nature of his meeting me there when he had almost decided not to brave the rainy, hour-long drive required to meet retired Yankees pitcher Ron Guidry, he shared with me the true object of his enthusiasm—his fight to get Thurman Munson recognized by the National Baseball Hall of Fame.

That fireball of a man was Tom Tunison.

He passionately regaled with me the statistics that put Munson in the same lofty status as his Hall of Fame contemporaries, Johnny Bench and Carlton Fisk. He gave me a copy of his well-researched pitch using advanced baseball metrics (WAR and WAR-10) that weren't available in Munson's day but are more finite means to measure a player's value to their team. I was impressed.

But I wasn't sure why this energetic stranger was lobbying ME on Munson's behalf. Sure, as John Kinsella, I had played a catcher, and I had worn a Yankees uniform in the film, but I certainly didn't have a lot of sway with Hall of Fame voters. My experience with so many fans from the movie over the years has taught me that I don't always need to know the reason WHY I am called upon to hear someone's story, just that it might offer them some inspiration to pursue their dream.

How many friends and strangers had inspired ME to leave my small-town farm and try to achieve my childhood dream of becoming an actor? Surely the odds were stacked against me. Yet, somehow, eight years later, I would return to a farm much like the one I grew up on to shoot a movie that would inspire a generation to pursue their inner voices much like Ray does in the film.

Beyond that—and I'm sure Tom knew that Thurman was born in Akron, Ohio— what he probably didn't know was that it was just 20 miles from the small, farm town I had grown up in. The site of Munson's tragic plane crash in 1979 was Akron-Canton Airport, one I have flown into many times myself.

Field of Dreams is really a movie about following your dreams and getting a second chance to right some wrongs. By the end of the film, Shoeless Joe gets to play baseball again, Terrence Mann is inspired to write again, Doc Graham finally gets his chance to bat against his heroes and, of course, Ray Kinsella gets to heal his relationship with his father.

Field of Dreams has taught me that there IS magic out there. It has taught me that sometimes even the most absurd dream is worth pursuing.

As Ray says to Terrence Mann, "There comes a time when all the cosmic tumblers have clicked into place, and the Universe opens itself up for a few seconds to show you what's possible."

Let's hope Tom's incredible journey will bring justice to another oversight by giving a great player whose career was shortened by tragedy the place he deserves in the Hall of Fame.

Listen to that Voice, Tom, and... go the distance.

As I See It

I have long believed that coincidences are calculated and measured moments that should be paid attention to and to be taken seriously. I have learned that remarkable outcomes based upon the level of response given to such moments are not so surprising. I have learned to recognize the most ordinary of signs life has provided and to follow them— one step at a time—and staying on course with an open mind and heart all the way to its end.

Of course it takes a great deal of faith to trust in the process and it may take some patience to stay the course. Faith because you believe. Patience because nothing can be forced, the next step comes to you in its own time.

Many years ago when my father-in-law died, my wife, Maureen and I stayed with her mother at her home. In the early morning hours the day of his funeral, Maureen rose quickly out of bed, said she couldn't sleep and needed to go out to the living room for some reason. She opened the curtains and at that very moment a furniture delivery truck rode past our parked car on the street, clipping off its rear-view mirror.

When the rest of us woke up later, she told the story to all of us—even how she was able to read the trucks painted company logo on its side panel as it whizzed by. We looked at that incident with absolute astonishment and wonder. We talked about the odds of her seeing it happen, how a few seconds more would have made for a different outcome, and how it was apparent to all of us that her dad had sent her a sign to go out to the living room at that exact moment in time. I spoke about it at his eulogy.

What has made telling the journey and story of Tom Tunison extra-special is that common denominator we share in such beliefs. That he has recognized the signs that life provides as something more than a coincidence, more than something you forget about and move on, that there is something greater at work you may not understand, but you're in it.

Tom Tunison never met Thurman Munson, but the bread crumbs left on the path of his life have aligned them together, an inexplicable partnership formed by the most unusual of circumstances, its long and winding road filled with an assortment of twists and turns to an uneven path that is loaded with remarkable outcomes "coincidence" sometimes provides. I know this because I was there with him throughout much of his later journey.

In every way, Tom Tunison's journey is both spiritual and inspiring. A journey taking decades to travel and decipher— and one he's still trying to figure out. Where we met was at a crossroads to his story. How we noticed, together, what was happening, couldn't be ignored. Our paths were meant to cross. Even how and when we met, well, we just couldn't ignore the signs.

It was a few years ago when I'd heard from a friend of mine living in Canton, Ohio, that a committee had been formed to campaign for Thurman Munson's induction into the National Baseball Hall of Fame and Museum in Cooperstown. Munson was from Ohio and lived in Canton with his wife Diana and three young children before his untimely and tragic death in 1979.

It just so happened that my friend— Dr. Jane Biehl—read about that committee in the local newspaper and sent me the article. Jane and I had partnered for years on another baseball Hall of Fame committee and she remembered I was a big New York Yankee fan.

What followed formed the beginning of two paths crossing— mine and Tom's— and widened the path he'd paved (and followed) in his search for baseball justice and immortality for Thurman Munson. From my initial involvement as the newest member of the committee, remarkable coincidence and equally remarkable opportunities occurred often, starting with our appearance on, *The Kara Conrad* television show in Binghamton, New York in 2018.

I'd contacted Kara soon after becoming a member of the Munson committee. We were looking to really branch out our reach— looking for some major publicity outside of Facebook and word-of-mouth. Being that I was from Binghamton and actually watched Munson play at Johnson Field as a member of the minor league Binghamton Triplets in 1968, I thought it was the perfect match for an interview. And I was right. Kara welcomed us in with open arms.

I won't get into the actual interview that occurred but suffice it to say it went very well. Tom was brilliant as the lead, proudly boasting of accomplishments and why Thurman should be in the Hall of Fame. We felt good about the interview as we left the studio together.

Tom had driven in from Bath, NY — a 90 minute drive— and I from my home in south Jersey. Following our interview, we decided ahead of time to spend the day together, starting with a visit to NYSEG stadium where the New York Mets minor league affiliate, "Rumble Ponies" played their home games.

I'd contacted Steve Popolski of the Mets a few weeks earlier and knew they were unveiling a mural that very day featuring many of the stars from Binghamton's minor league past— including Thurman Munson. That was coincidence enough that it was happening just a few hours after our interview day and that we'd be among the first people to lay eyes on it. And while we joked that it was a cool coincidence, what happened next was yet another in a string of those remarkable "coincidences" that had us shaking our heads— and giving thanks at the same time.

I called Steve and put him on speaker phone as we drove to the stadium. He seemed a little anxious and said, "We're taping segments with people on our Booster Club today, quotes about every player on the mural. People can listen to what is being said about the players as they look at the mural. It's a big deal and we've been working on it for some time."

"Can we watch?" I asked.

Steve paused then said, "Well, there's a bit of a problem that's come up. It seems like the person we had asked to talk about Thurman Munson didn't work out and can't make it in and today is our only day to tape... we were hoping you and Tom could do it."

Tom took a good look at me and smiled in utter disbelief. "We'll be right there," I said.

Later in the story you'll find out more about that day from Tom's perspective. But it was at that point when we realized something bigger than us was at work here, that there was something unusual going on. And as the months have passed and we've grown closer like brothers, the "coincidences" have grown and the path has widened.

The title, "Go the Distance," is taken from one of the most powerful baseball movies ever made— "Field of Dreams." These three whispered words, "Go the distance," that Kevin Costner's character kept hearing in his head has defined also Tom Tunison's quest. And while that quest to, *go the distance* remains a work-in-progress, we hope you enjoy this part of the journey.

-Gary Kaschak
1/1/2022

"THURMAN"

If I could relive a Yankees baseball moment
If I could go back in time
I would be watching THURMAN MUNSON when he was in his prime
I'd say "That's how you do it,
Yes, that's the way it's done,
You take the field with purpose
You hit the ball and run.

I wouldn't catch him loafing
To him that would be a sin
He played the game with focus and he played the game to win
He might hit one to DEATH VALLEY, 463 feet away
I've already seen him do it
On one bright October day
His Jersey will be all dirty

It simply has to be
Nothing is going to stop him
In his quest for victory
He'll argue with the umpire
He'll shout and yell and scream
But when the fuss is over
He only did it for his team

Because when you are CAPTAIN
And the leader of the band
You don't pull any punches
And you ALWAYS make a stand
And when the game is over
And it's time for us to go
I'll say, "That THURMAN MUNSON... he gave us quite a show,"

I didn't get a picture
No, he didn't even sign
But that's OKAY because...
I just watched THURMAN MUNSON in his PRIME

    Thomas J. Tunison
    August, 2018

Chapter 1
Perthes & The Rubber Ball

"I felt a sudden, searing pain in my knee, but thought nothing of it and said nothing to my friends."

When I was about six years old I was just like any other normal kid my age. Playing with my friends outside when the weather was nice or staying inside when it was cold or rainy was about the extent of our daily choices.

Being inside all day wasn't a bad thing, it just wasn't like being outdoors where I could run and ride bikes with my friends. I loved the outdoors because I loved to run. I have it on good authority that I was the fastest kid in my age group in the neighborhood, even faster than some of the older boys and girls. And with our bustling Bellmore, Long Island neighborhood of up to 100 kids playing and running around all day in the summer months, that's saying something.

I remember how running felt so special to me. To go all out and be ahead of my friends when we'd race in the streets or even on our bikes was the greatest feeling of all. Of course I liked winning any game we'd play, but running just did it for me. I really liked the way it made me feel. To taste the wind on my face. To feel the sun against my skin. To shake the snow from my boots. It didn't matter the season. I would run no matter what, come rain, come shine or come high water and a foot of snow. I felt as fast as a racehorse and as strong as an ox and on top of the world when I ran. I was fast, in, fastest boy around. Strong in, never getting tired strong. Running around wherever I chose to run gave me a freedom like no other. And running was what I did best. They said I was on the fast track to becoming the fastest kid ever from our area— maybe even the fastest runner in history— but time was going to take care of all that. We'd see.

I've talked to other people about having memories at that young age and they seem surprised at what I remember. I wondered why that was so I looked it up on the internet and read that you can't really process long-term-memories up to age six, something to do with brain development at that age. Nowhere did it say it was impossible to remember things that far back, and it didn't matter to me if it did. I remember things down to the details. I don't know, maybe it's because of what happened to me back then. I don't know. All I can tell you is what I remember, and I remember a lot from those days, and that the big memories- THE BIG MEMORIES- were about to take hold and stay with me to this day. I remember that day in 1969 as if it were yesterday.

I was racing bikes with my friends, Jimmy Donachie and Eddie Short, then racing against them on foot, a customary routine that never got old for any of us. I felt a sudden, searing pain in my knee, but thought nothing of it and said nothing to my friends. The pain stayed on for a while and would go away, but kept coming back. I wanted to ignore it but I couldn't. It hurt. When I got home later that day I rubbed that knee and wished the pain away. It didn't seem as bad when I was just walking, but still the pain was there. I went to bed that night without telling my parents and prayed that night for the pain to go away for good.

The next day everything seemed back to normal for a while. I was moving around the house like I always did, and the pain seemed to have left. So off I went back to the streets with my friends, running and biking like any other day. But as soon as I started running, that same awful pain had returned, only sharper and more severe. I stopped running after just a few feet and rubbed my leg again. I still didn't want my friends knowing what was happening to me, but I couldn't go on any further. I must have made some excuse up and probably told them I had to go home early that day for some family function, and so I left.

Still, I didn't say a word to anyone, not even my parents. I was a little scared and very confused, but when the pain moved into my hip and I started limping, people began to take notice. The hobbling was something

I couldn't hide or control no matter how hard I tried. And anytime I tried walking normally, an enormous pressure and that blistering pain took over. Maybe I had a broken bone or something like that, or strained a muscle that would take a few days to heal. Either way I knew my parents would find out soon enough. And just like I thought, it didn't take long at all.

At first we all thought I might have twisted an ankle or even broken a bone in my leg, but the problem persisted, grew worse, and I was having difficulty walking— even doing normal things like walking from one room to another. The pain had gone from sometimes to always and my parents took notice. And when I limped just a few feet before taking a break, my parents decided to have a consultation with Dr. Caso.

A series of tests and x-rays were next, and despite the results from those tests, more tests were needed. And after a few weeks of trying to pin down what the issue was, the grim discovery had been made— I had a rare degenerative hip disease called Perthes Disease. It was a mouthful for sure— a disease none of us had ever heard of— and certainly not the news we were prepared to hear.

Turns out Perthes was an awful thing to have. The ball in my hip joint had deteriorated to such a point that only two options to treat it were discussed— and neither sounded good. Surgery was the first option, but there was no guarantee the problem would be solved. Option two was to stay off my feet— *for three years*— and it came with very specific, life-altering instructions to be followed in a very specific order.

Our orthopedic specialist, Dr. Trinkle, didn't believe surgery was the answer. His plan and recommendation was to keep me off my feet as much as possible, to keep taking x-rays and hope for the best. And as he talked to my parents about the grim choice they had to make and what it could mean even at the end of three years, words like, crippled, and may never walk normally again, were mentioned. That the first step in the healing process included a full-body cast to be fitted and worn for up to a year or more, followed by a wheelchair for another year and crutches for yet another. Oh, and no guarantees either way.

Being so young I had no say in the matter and wasn't privy to those conversations. I really didn't know what was going on or really understood what I'd be up against. I didn't really understand what was about to happen to me, how I'd need to rely on my parents and siblings and friends for everything. My little six-year old brain couldn't really comprehend that I wouldn't be able to play outside with friends, that I'd be a lump for at least year, and that I'd need help washing my body, getting dressed and yes... even going to the bathroom.

I'm sure it was a shock to my parents and my siblings. My parents had to have been told the sacrifices they'd have to make for me, how much constant care I'd need— especially that first year— all the while under the notion that it may not work out in the end. I'm sure they had great concerns for me, that I'd be losing some prime years from my youth. That active little Tommy might be ignored by friends who could run and ride and play ball all day. That I may even become depressed, lonely or anxious. In the end, after all the talk and the tears and trying to figure out life for me, the full body cast was decided upon by all parties.

But I was six and had no real concept of time. And I don't ever recall feeling lonely or depressed throughout when I was first fitted for that white suit of armor. Sure, I wanted to stay out there with my friends and do all the things I'd done before. That was a given that I wanted to run again and do the same things I'd always done. Now I had to do what they told me to do and go from there. I'd have to just go with the flow and show some courage.

Before this all happened I was just a normal kid in the kindergarten with my friends and just assumed I'd be going into the first grade along with them. I hadn't put it all together yet that I'd be bed-ridden and be home-schooled. Life was changing, and changing real fast.

I remember my first night in the hospital after having that body cast fit to me. I looked like the Mummy and was as stiff as one. I recall lying on my back, the extra weight of the cast making it hard to move freely, when my stomach began hurting. The pain was excruciating, and I started crying. When the nurse came down a really dark hallway to check on me, I was relieved. She spent a few minutes with me and I told her what was wrong. She assured me the problem would be fixed. Several minutes later I heard another set of footsteps coming down the hallway. My bed was right next to a door with a high glass window, so I could see the big figure of Dr. Trinkle coming around the corner.

He carried an electric saw that really startled me. He didn't say much as he got closer to me, then with a half-smile started cutting a hole on the cast near my stomach area. I could hear the drill the whole time like I was in a dentist's office, and I was petrified. I thought that if he made any mistake or flinched just a little he could cut my stomach open! I was helpless watching bits and pieces of the hardened cast flying around the room, praying that I wouldn't see my own skin and bones start flying around the room. I couldn't move. I was frozen in fear, just waiting for the whole ordeal to end.

I'm sure my motionless body helped Dr. Trinkle's aim, and before long, he turned off the saw, the noise had ended and he smiled down at the work he'd just done—he knew what he was doing after all. Suddenly my stomach could expand and I could breath normally again. It was huge relief, but something had already gone wrong and this was only day one. I tried not to think about it, but I did. I wondered if they'd need to cut out more openings, or if what just happened was a one time thing. I didn't want to be scared like that again, thinking about the pain had the saw missed its mark. It was a lot to think about.

They ended up taking x-rays all the time, just like they said they would. But I was in the hospital only a few nights before I was sent home where most of my recovery was done. Being the youngest of seven kids, my parents had an awful lot already to manage in our household. It's hard to imagine managing so many kids at once, but I think we all kind of took it for granted because it was all we knew. There were lots of big families like ours, so it felt like no big deal at the time. But thinking back on it now, it's hard to imagine trying to juggle the needs of such a big family with me needing round-the-clock care.

It was pretty easy to do what I was told because I couldn't even move. My cast started at the chest and went all the way down to my stomach and around the back to the hip and then down my right leg completely. I know it had to have been a tremendous amount of work taking care of me. They would bathe me by hand and I had to use a bedpan instead of a toilet. And

I would get constipated and needed enemas because I wasn't able to digest my food properly. Just laying there not being able to do anything as natural as going to the bathroom on your own was rough and embarrassing. Losing your dignity is the worst. I had such great support from my six siblings and my parents constantly were there doting on me. I was very, very fortunate to have that support system and is something I'll never forget.

When I got back home, they'd set up my bed in the living room to better keep an eye on me. I didn't know what "invalid" meant, but I was pretty close to being one. I could move my arms and upper body but not being able to move properly from below my waste line made me feel like a prisoner in my own body. I read my comic books, did some drawings, filled-in my coloring books and some homework, but none of that replaced the empty feeling I had by not being able to run outside and play with my friends. I needed something more to do that would pass the time and entertain me. That's when I spotted a rubber ball on the floor and asked one of my siblings to bring it to me.

I started throwing that ball into the air and spinning it with my right hand when it came down, then doing it again and again and never wanted stop. And I got good at it— really good. I found out soon enough to either catch it on its way down or risk having it bounce across the floor away from my reach.

And as I got better I started counting how many times I'd throw that ball to myself before missing one. I became so good at it, I rarely missed. And I never felt bored. I had my rubber ball and the make-believe games I'd play with it. I was happy to have it and happy to be doing something with a ball. Sometimes I'd just spin that ball over and over with my right hand. When the weather was warmer, they placed a cot outside on the lawn where I'd continue my "Throwing game."

I must have thrown that ball into the air a million times. Up and down all day long, tossing and spinning, tossing and spinning. My little game had started to turn into something bigger, I just didn't know it at the time.

Little did I know that following the path of that ball helped sharpen my hand-eye coordination skills. Little did I know that thousands of repetitions from that up and down motion would help me later become a better ballplayer. And little did I know that the constant counting and keeping track of how many times I caught that ball in a row formed the beginning to my curiosity in baseball statistics— one that would become an exploration and then an obsession and would one day lead me all the way to the doors of Cooperstown.

Chapter 2
The Connection

"I may have felt trapped being in my body cast, but I felt free watching Thurman play."

About a year earlier I started becoming interested in major league baseball and especially to the New York Yankees. It was a natural match because my three brothers were Yankee fans and seemed to always be talking about them. I heard them mentioning great Yankee names all the time, and every time I heard one of those great names come up, it just became engrained in my mind.

But it wasn't just the names, and that they were names on my team that so interested me, it was *how* their names sounded to me that would draw me to them. Even then I thought how some of them were so unusual sounding, that they became easy for me to remember and to identify with them as Yankee greats. Babe Ruth, Lou Gehrig, Mickey Mantle, Yogi Berra and Whitey Ford were different sounding names for me. They really sounded so unusual compared to most other names from the other teams, and the fact that they were all Yankees had to mean something.

I was still too young to be interested in or to even understand baseball standings or its statistics, or to even know what a World Series was, but in listening to my brothers, the Yankees had been in a lot of them. I was still an infant when the Dodgers swept the Yankees in the 1963 World Series, and a toddler a year later when the Yanks lost to the Cardinals in seven games. By the time I started paying attention to what my brothers were saying, the Yankees had begun an unprecedented free fall in the standings—finishing 6th in the 10 team American League in 1965, an unheard of last place finish in 1966 and just a ninth place finish in 1967—my first year, if you will, following baseball as much as a four-and-a-half year old could— then bounced back in 1968 with at least a winning record for the first time in four years.

It was right around the same time my Perthes diagnosis was discovered when Mickey Mantle announced his retirement in March of that year. I didn't understand what retirement was and didn't care to know what it meant, but during spring training and the start of that 1969 season my brothers had plenty to say about the new look Yankees. While they sounded off about the Yankees chances of winning another pennant, I was more interested in hearing the names of players on the roster, the newer Yankees and a few holdovers from a year or two earlier. I wanted to hear their names spoken so I could process in my own way who would become the next stars for the Yankees.

They talked about Joe Pepitone, Jake Gibbs, Mel Stottlemyre and Horace Clarke— names that weren't quite in the same category as my big four, yet still had that Yankee sounding name to what I believed a Yankee name should be. Pepitone sounded like an Italian dish of some kind, Jake Gibbs was simple, was easy to say; Mel Stottlemyre, well, I couldn't even pronounce his name and I thought Horace was *horse* and wondered why a person would be named after any animal.

I remember listening to Phil Rizzuto on the Yankee broadcasts speak about all the old timers he played with and against, and when he'd mention them my mind would take off and I'd imagine what each of them looked like when they played. Whitey Ford and Yogi Berra had retired just a few years earlier so I never got to see them play, but Rizzuto told stories about Mantle, Joe DiMaggio— both teammates of his— and plenty of stories about Babe Ruth— some bigger than life. I loved that he talked about those players like he did. Being bed-ridden allowed for plenty of time to listen and to let my imagination run free with images of Babe Ruth hitting a ball a million feet, or pointing to center-field in a World Series game, then hitting a home run over the wall on the next pitch. These were indelible images that began with the storytelling words of Rizzuto, then straight to my minds eye that churned words into pictures and pictures into newsreel— images that have stayed with me all these years later.

I first heard the name, *Thurman Munson* when he suddenly appeared in the Yankee lineup in early August. I had no idea where he came from and had no understanding of the minor league systems, but I was glued to the little black and white TV dad had set up for me on our porch. Rizzuto talked about the great Yankee catchers like Yogi and Elston Howard and Bill Dickey before introducing Munson and I took notice to *Dickey* and *Elston* and thought both were perfect Yankee names. Then when Rizzuto said, *Thurman Munson* for the first time and said he was a catcher, I immediately aligned *Thurman* alongside *Dickey* and *Elston* and *Yogi* into becoming my newest Big Four Yankees. And even though Babe and Whitey and Yogi and Mickey were perfect sounding Yankee names, *Thurman Munson* went straight to the head of that class for me, on the spot.

He was just starting out, hadn't even had his first at bat, but that didn't matter to me. In my impressionable mind I equated success with the name and Thurman had them all beat. Maybe nobody else knew that or thought the way I did, but it was a fact and it could get no better than *Thurman Munson*, and maybe, just maybe, he was going to become the next Mickey Mantle.

I so knew in my heart he'd become a Yankee great because of that name. I kept repeating to myself, *Thurman Munson, Thurman Munson, Thurman Munson* like it was a broken record. I didn't know anyone named Thurman and had never heard it before and if I said it fast enough it almost sounded like, *Herman Munster*— a character from a TV show my family watched when I was very young.

It may sound like a corny reason to latch onto a player like that, but it was really no different than someone following a team because of a uniform or helmet or team logo they thought was cool. *Thurman Munson* would be my guy from that point on.

As Rizzuto spoke about the catching position in Yankee history, Thurman worked a walk against his future teammate, "Catfish" Hunter, then collected his first big league hit later in the game and lined a sharp single to right to score two runners in the eighth. I was in absolute awe.

It wasn't just the walk and the two hits that had me so drawn to Thurman. It was the way he played the game— it seemed different to me.

You could tell right away there was an excitement to the team when he got behind the plate or up to bat. He was just that type of player. His body language and demeanor set the stage. He wasn't afraid of any pitcher or player and you could see that on his face and the way he carried himself. He played hard, and he played to win. He blocked the plate on close plays at home, not backing down an inch to the likes of George Scott, Boog Powell and Dick Allen. And when the dust would settle after those future collisions at the plate, he always came up with the ball, on his back, ball in the air for the umpire to see.

I loved watching Yankee games but now I had more reason to. I had something bigger and better to look forward to now, and couldn't wait for the next Yankee telecast to air so I could see Thurman Munson again. And it didn't matter if he was batting or on defense. I could see him either way, especially when the center-field camera was used.

While I was fixated on Thurman Munson, across town, it was the other New York team— the National League Mets—who captured the attention of New Yorkers and captivated the entire world of baseball during that 1969 year.

I have vivid memories of watching the Mets in 1969 and remember them winning the World Series and Cleon Jones making the final catch. I liked the Mets, but I loved the Yankees. I remember that Mets team and roster and the excitement and euphoria surrounding them on the road to one of the most unlikely championships in baseball history.

They called it a "Miracle" that they'd won and I never understood until years later, when I learned more about baseball history and began understanding how hard it was for any team to win. That the Mets beat the highly favored Orioles with Frank and Brooks Robinson would teach me a lesson about sports and life that has always stayed with me, that no matter how it looks on paper, the games are played between the lines by real people.

That first year of my recovery turned out to be one of the most interesting and memorable years in modern sports history— especially for fans of New York teams. The Mets had been the laughing stock of baseball since coming into the league in 1962— losing 100 games just about every season— and never posing a serious popularity threat to what the Yankees had built. Despite all that, the Mets became the darlings of New York, but being in a household of Yankees fans, I hardly paid any attention to the Mets all that time. When I got older I heard a sports album recorded in the early 70's where Curt Gowdy said that, "The Keystone Cops were alive and well and playing baseball at Shea Stadium." And that was true up until 1969.

Then Willis Reed and Walt Frazier led the New York Knicks to the National Basketball Association championship, and a brash young quarterback named Joe Namath led his New York Jets to another unlikely football championship against another heavily favored Baltimore team— all in that same season of sports.

I'd seen Joe Namath a few times at Dr. Trinkle's office, getting his fragile knees looked at. I wanted to say something to him but never did. I read about Namath years later, how he partied all the time into the wee hours of the morning and led a fast-paced life. And he came across with an arrogance that shocked many writers. Even when football's most-eligible bachelor quarterback pulled into a Miami hotel driving a turquoise Cadillac prior to the Super Bowl, he spoke to the media and guaranteed that his Jets— despite Vegas favoring the strait-laced, all-business, Hall of Fame headed, passing-legend Johnny Unitas's Colts by a mere 18 points— would win the game.

The Colts had blown through the NFL that season, losing only to Cleveland a year earlier. Despite losing only one game as well, they hadn't made the playoffs—an odd misfortune in the annals of league history. With nothing yet to show for two seasons with a combined two losses, the Colts didn't need additional motivational support handed them by Namath's breaking an unwritten, ill-advised rule to say nothing to fire up and inspire an opponent.

But whatever motivation Broadway Joe handed to the Colts on a silver platter never manifested on the field. The crystal ball that Namath apparently had looked into and with just enough slingshot-precision passing performance on the field took down the Goliath of the rival league.

A star that had been born had been born again. Bigger than the Beatles. Bigger than life. Final score, Jets 16, Colts 7.

That Namath backed his words and took down the class of the NFL, and the Mets beat the highly favored class of the American League was sports irony at its finest. New York over Baltimore in two sports. It really was A Tale of Two Cities.

It was such an important time in every way, not just for sports in New York, but for our country and the world. It was just a year earlier when Robert Kennedy and Martin Luther King were killed in cold blood and The Vietnam war had divided the country. Then in August of 1969, 400,000 people converged onto a small farm in upstate New York for the Woodstock Festival, and a month earlier an astronaut named Neil Armstrong led his Apollo 11 crew on a historic mission, an unbelievable event in the annals of space exploration by putting a man on the moon for the first time.

I've wondered, on the occasion of a full moon, if my parents ever stared at that same moon right after the Apollo 11 crew landed on its surface, contemplating the irony in Neil Armstrong's, "One giant step for man, one giant leap for mankind," and wondered if their little Tommy would ever walk again.

But I was still too young to understand any of what was going on in the world and how any of it mattered. I was too young to really process those events. Aside from recovering from Perthes and getting out of my body cast, what mattered to me most now was the Yankees and Thurman Munson. Even with all the other New York teams bringing championships to the city and the Yankees falling on hard times, I couldn't be pulled away from them. Phil Rizzuto spoke about their rich history all the time, and it fascinated me.

The Mets had been around for less than a decade and didn't appeal as much to me. I'm sure most young boys or girls living in the New York area likely would have gravitated to the Mets with Mickey retired and the Yankee glory days behind them. I think it was Rizzuto who early on would say, "This boy Thurman Munson is something else," and he drilled that message all the time. And he was right, he was something else.

And it wasn't only Rizzuto who noticed how special Thurman was. The other Yankee announcer, Bill White, praised his game all the time. And whether it was getting a big hit or throwing out a runner or even stealing a base, Thurman Munson did it with a flair like no other player I'd seen to that point. He hustled on every play. His uniform was always dirty. He seemed to be in control of every game, of every pitch. I couldn't get enough of watching him play.

I loved Munson. He was my guy hitting the heck out of the ball and leading the way behind the plate. You knew this guy was the leader, who could beat you in so many ways, it was like watching nobody else until I saw Pete Rose years later, both of them played, "Take no prisoners," baseball and Thurman played it clean. He played hard and got along with other players, often joking with them at the plate. He was just a special player.

The way Thurman Munson played the game was important to me to look up to someone who never came out of a game and never wanted to. I'd already witnessed his rough and tumble ways that sometimes led to an injury, but he never came out of the game. He was my favorite player and always would be. He was a star amongst stars, playing with abandonment, seemingly in on every play.

I may have felt trapped being in my body cast, but I felt free when I watched Thurman play. He had a hold on me that made me want to get out there again, not to let any injury of any kind get in my way. I was just six and a half years old, and while my mind was still developing and processing information, I felt so connected to Thurman Munson in ways I could never explain.

Chapter 3
From Body Cast to Wheelchair

"I loved that card because it captured Thurman Munson in an instant, blocking the plate, mask off, ball in glove, seemingly unconcerned with the thrashing spikes from the runner as he flopped onto home plate."

My full-body cast became my uniform for that entire year and then into 1970, and my parents and six siblings doted on me whenever they needed to.

I was the baby of the family, the last of the Tunison army my parents had created. All four boys and three girls were healthy, loving and cared for each other. I shared one bedroom with my three older brothers Bob, Roy and Tim, and my sisters Debbie, Ginnie and Lori did the same. There was one-and-a-half bathrooms, an unfinished basement, and all the normal rooms a house has. It was tight, only I didn't know it.

I attended school for Kindergarten before the problem arose, then I was home schooled for the first and second grades. The second grade teacher thought I should skip third grade and go right into fourth, but my parents said no, they wanted me to be with the same kids of my age.

Of course I wasn't thrilled with needing so much care and attention. I just wanted to run around like my friends could at will. But knowing it was out of the question for now was really not bothering me too much because my friend Jimmy Donachie was always there too cheer me up. I'm told on good authority that I was pretty understanding about the whole thing, and at the many appointments I had with Dr. Trinkle, I never really got upset or sulked around. Over the course of that year I'd always heard the same thing about how I was making good progress and what a good boy I was, but my circumstances hadn't changed. I went to each appointment hoping to hear otherwise, but the words I wanted to hear most from Dr. Trinkle weren't said.

By summer, nothing had changed, with the exception that they set up a cot on our front lawn for me where I continued playing my "Throwing game." But no longer could I simply shout for help if my ball bounced away, or wait a minute or two for someone to walk by. Being outside was wonderful, but accuracy mattered more than ever. If it had been at all possible for me to have improved the accuracy I'd demonstrated inside the house to the great outdoors, I'd probably become the most accurate ball tosser of all time. At least that's what I thought I was. But the possibilities of error had increased dramatically. With no ceiling restricting how high a ball could be tossed, I challenged myself. I threw higher and higher and pretended to be an outfielder or an infielder making the catch. I counted the outs made in a single game— 27 for both sides— and began a new game of catch 54. No runs, no hits and especially, no errors.

I think I did pretty good for myself, thinking back on it now, even though everyone knew me as, "The Crippled Kid." Not that they made fun of me because they didn't. The neighborhood kids were really good to me. There really were 100 or so kids in our neighborhood and it was something that you'd always have pickup games of any kind going on. Stickball, wiffle-ball, pinky-ball, hide-and-go-seek, Kick The Can, tag. And it went on all day and night… only I was missing out. But what I wasn't missing out on was the continued development of Thurman Munson and my Yankees.

Thurman had played at the end of that 1969 season as if he were the starting every day catcher over Jake Gibbs, Frank Fernandez and even fellow rookie Johnny Ellis. I'd watched about all the Yankee games that year and their rotation of catchers in and out of the lineup reminded me of the pitchers who went every four games. Then when Thurman started playing it seemed to be him in most games.

But by the end of spring training, Fernandez was dealt to Oakland for Danny Cater, Ellis was shifted to first base and Gibbs became backup to the one and only Thurman Munson. I had no clue how baseball transactions were made or decided on, or how decisions impacted the career of a player. All I knew was Thurman Munson was the starting catcher for the New York Yankees and it made me happy.

With all the talk around New York still centered on the Mets, few had noticed an improving and exciting Yankee team. New players like Roy White and Bobby Murcer had me excited that they were Thurman's teammates, and that all three would one day become Yankee legends and heroes of mine, or that Bobby Murcer— and not Thurman Munson—-had been anointed as Mickey Mantle's replacement.

That all made sense when Rizzuto explained that both were from Oklahoma, both had been shortstops when they first came up and both were moved to centerfield— a position of unparalleled Yankee greatness since 1936. It seemed natural to management and Yankee fans alike that such a continuation that began with Joe Dimaggio then was passed down to Mickey would default right on cue into a promising youngster named Bobby Murcer. After all, Murcer had clubbed 26 home runs in his rookie season of 1969, led the club in runs batted in, was only 23 years old and played a good center field.

I didn't know at the time how unfair that was to Bobby Murcer, or what his role would one day be in the days following Thurman's death. I had no clue what Divine Intervention was, or anything to do with spirituality— that was all years ahead of me. All I knew was I liked all three players.

Thurman, Bobby and Roy all had great seasons for my new look Yankees. Bobby led the club in home runs, Roy in runs batted in and Thurman the team leader in batting average— good for eighth in the entire league and two points above the cherished threshold of .3oo set by the games best hitters. As if it weren't enough, Thurman was named American League Rookie of the Year for 1970, a unanimous decision save the one vote cast for Cleveland's Roy Foster.

Of course I knew this was a good thing for Thurman— a great thing for him—but had little understanding of any awards and the like. I always listened to my brothers talk about such things, and paid attention to their opinions and knowledge of the game. They spoke of Stan Bahnsen winning it just a few years ago, and Tom Tresh a few years before that. And as they read from the paper all the past winners of the award there was no mention of Babe Ruth, Mickey Mantle, Whitey Ford, or Yogi Berra. And while I wasn't aware that the award hadn't been introduced into baseball long after Ruth's rookie season, there was no doubt in my mind this was something special.

I paid little attention to non-Yankees as my brothers read the entire list of past winners. We had no way of knowing that the previous years winner and the winner the year after Thurman won would one day team up to win back-to-back World Series titles, that Lou Piniella and Chris Chambliss would become key parts on those great Yankee teams. All I knew was Thurman Munson had just accomplished something none of the great Yankees ever had.

While all this was going on in Yankee land, Dr. Trinkle had me in for another routine follow-up, but this was far from routine. At first he examined me like he always had, then put down his instruments, looked at me and my mother and said, "It's time… time to remove your body cast."

I looked at my mother and could hardly believe my ears. I remember feeling exhilarated when Dr. Trinkle started cutting into it. He began right at the exact spot the night he sawed into it to relieve the pressure I was feeling. But I wasn't nervous like I was then. I was excited and couldn't wait for it to come apart, couldn't wait for Dr. Trinkle to do his work and to feel a freedom I hadn't had for a year. I wanted to see my stomach again, to feel my hands go across it, to rub it and to scratch it. I wanted to be able to bend down and touch my toes, to put my hands on my hips and just feel my body again.

It took little time for the cast to split into two pieces and fall to the floor. I have no idea how much the thing weighed, but I felt like a bird—almost weightless—and even light enough to fly, almost like a feather.

But it was awkward at first. My body needed more time to acclimate to the sitting position, and because certain muscles had atrophied, standing or walking was difficult for me. I'd learned that an idol body was sort of in hibernation during all that time and needed quite a lot of stimulation and movement in order to get back to some form of normalcy. I'd been surprised at how weak my legs had become during that time in bed, my leg muscles looking more like sticks that wobbled and didn't balance properly. It was then I was told that the wheelchair would be necessary as the next stage of my recovery— and instead of lying in bed for a year, I'd be sitting up.

I don't remember being told earlier about the wheelchair or that I'd need to be in one for another year. I don't recall feeling sad or upset or even if I cried. Being bed-ridden for a full year gave me some understanding of what an entire year actually was, and now I'd have to do it again.

I have no bad memories of what I felt like going from body cast to wheelchair, but it was true, my muscles had receded and sitting was far different that lying down flat. The angle my blood circulated had changed, and frequent rubdowns and massages were needed. But in short order, I was back at it, throwing that rubber ball into the air and inventing newer games that always involved that little ball. Sitting was a whole lot better than lying flat on my back.

There was a new set of rules I needed to follow and pay close attention to. I'd followed the rules they gave me when I was in my body cast, but I really had no choice. Being in a suit of armor really restricted my movements, so even if I'd been tempted to get out of bed, I couldn't. The body cast rules were easy to follow.

But now I had some freedom, and that's what they were afraid of. When Dr. Trinkle warned me I couldn't stand, walk or kneel, that any or all would ruin any progress made from that first year, well, I took notice. Of course I was anxious to do all three, but I was scared at what he told me, and knew I had to listen to everything he said. There I was, six years old, being warned firmly and needing to have extreme discipline for such a little boy. I followed these rules even to the point of disobeying my mother one time— a stomach ache so bad that in the middle of the night I had to call out for her.

I'd entertained the idea of getting up by myself but I hadn't done that yet. And I knew if I did get up my mother would hear me. It was such a helpless feeling, but I'd followed the rules early on and wouldn't dare stand or try to even crawl to the bathroom by myself.

So my mom picked me up out of bed and ran to the bathroom demanding that I stand next to the toilet and not throw up all over the floor. I was torn as to what I should do, and as I tried to hold it all in, I screamed, "NO!"

She took hold of me and started crying just then— I think she realized at that moment what she had asked of me, and that I was being true to the instructions from Dr. Trinkle, fearful any move would setback my recovery, that I'd further damage my hips and bones.

I think I started getting a little bit more rambunctious after that. Sure, I was scared I could have messed things up, and I knew I had to follow the rules, but I was just a kid with kids thoughts and somethings kids thoughts could lead to trouble. I was being tutored at my friend Eddie Short's house one day and had one of those mischievous thoughts come to mind. I'd been left alone in the house for a short time waiting for Eddie to come home from school when I was staring out the window, so badly wanting to go outside and play. I studied the surrounding area and noticed a telephone pole and maple tree so close together, that I'd be able to climb up the telephone pole and get myself into the tree.

When Eddie arrived home I explained my plan, and, kids being kids, I made my move. Once I got into the tree and felt safe and secure, I grabbed a tree branch and was pulled from the tree— still hanging onto that limb for dear life.

There was a good eight foot drop from where I dangled and I was in a real predicament. I could drop to the ground and that likely would set back my progress by years, or even damage myself for life, or hang on to that bending branch until help came along. That last one was really my only choice.

Eddie ran to my house and got my brother Roy's attention. Roy raced from our house, stood below me and pulled me to safety, wrapping me in his arms and giving me a well-deserved scolding. I don't remember if Roy ever told our parents, but that incident didn't seem to change my ways.

As I grew accustomed to the wheelchair I started experimenting with it. With no traction below my waistline, all that were my arms, and as time went on and I learned to pivot and turn and navigate, I felt confident enough to join— and challenge— my good friends, Jimmy Donachie and Eddie Short, to a race, me against them on their Big Wheel bicycles.

So I'd race them down the street in my wheelchair. I don't recall winning or not, but I was back in the game, improvising and participating as best I could. I'm not sure how I got away with it without my parents consent, but we raced many times down our street.

I'm pretty sure that kind of exercise helped develop my biceps and shoulders, and later the crutches made me even stronger. In fact, I remember sitting on the ground totally free of my wheelchair, and I'd scoot across the floor with my arms in front and shoot myself across the floor. I got so quick doing that, my siblings used to try and race me. I even did that on the lawn when my friends would come over and play and they would play the games my way, including our favorite— a baseball game by scooting around on our butts, just to make sure I was a part of things.

They'd take me down to the curb some days where I'd pitch wiffle balls to my friends from my chair. For anyone not familiar with a wiffle ball, it has some sort of a mind of its own—almost like a knuckleball does. With a series of slats carved into each ball, the wind would take it and it would never go straight and because of that nobody knew how to control one.

But from all the practice and all the times I'd watched games on TV, I developed a "riser" that started low to the ground— maybe six inches from the ground— that would rise another six inches just before it reached the batter. The fact that nobody ever made contact with that pitch made me think that one day when I was able to run and play again, that maybe I should become a pitcher.

By the summer of 1971, I'd been on that wheelchair for half a year and had grown tired of it. I was eight years old going on nine and started to really feel the itch to abandon my wheelchair and finish up the final stage on a set of crutches, then onto a freedom I longed for.

But I knew there were no guarantees because I'd overheard those conversations between Dr. Trinkle and my parents. But I wasn't worried or concerned— there was a gentle peace I felt all along— that things were going to be just fine, that I'd recover, that I'd be a boy again, that my time would come.

I'd grown tired of the wheelchair, but not of baseball. I went to a lot of my brothers Little league baseball games with my dad. He'd load me up in the car and I was just thrilled, totally enthralled with the games and everything about it, especially watching my brother Tim run the bases. It was right at that time I started getting interested in collecting baseball cards.

There was just something about a baseball card and the 10 card pack it came in that put you over the top. A dime was all one cost, but a dime wasn't always easy to come by. I think that's part of the mystique we shared back then, that ten cents wasn't always easy to come by and when you had it, the appreciation for a pack of baseball cards was real.

Of course we'd chew the pack bonus of a long stick of pink bubble gum until it went stale— usually no more than a minute or two, then rifled thought the pack like our life depended on it, searching for a favorite player or one you may not have. I'd spend hours looking at the cards, studying the statistics and comments on the back.

I really wanted to learn what all those numbers meant, and as I got some help and began understanding categories like batting averages and earned run averages, I learned what was great, what was good and what was poor. I'd learned fractions long before taught any algebra classes that were still years away. I was way ahead of my peers when it came to math and always enjoyed solving numbers problems, and baseball statistics was no exception.

When the morning paper was delivered to our house every day I reviewed the boxscores from the previous days games. Without a calculator in the house I taught myself mostly through long division and multiplication how some statistics were arrived at, and within a few years understood the rest. From that point on I often pulled out a pencil and paper and went to work on team standings, batting averages and even began "inventing" some new stats combining runs scored and runs batted in. Before long, I began memorizing some of the easier numbers and broke down numbers into its closest whole-number fraction, reducing that number down to its smallest fraction. I could blurt out a teams winning percentage and come close or be exact just hearing its record, and the same went for any batting average calculation when given hits and at bats from any given player.

Aside from looking at player images when I first started collecting baseball cards in 1971, I'd flip the cards over and I'd study— and memorize— the lifetime statistics of every player. I collected cards for years after that, and that 1971 Topps cards set became my favorite set and still is— especially the Thurman Munson with the black border— one I kept getting in the packs I opened.

I remember taking a thicker rubber band for the cards I didn't care so much about that would take more of a beating, and wrapped a much thinner rubber band around my favorite cards — the Munson, Roy White and Bobby Murcer cards—then placed them in shoe boxes like everybody else did. Years later my mom gave them all away to my cousins daughter. Oh well.

I loved that card because it captured Thurman Munson in an instant, blocking the plate, mask off, ball in glove, seemingly unconcerned with the thrashing spikes from the runner as he flopped onto home plate. And there he was, right down in the dirt with the runner, ball in hand.

Thurman Munson was a warrior, a fierce competitor and such a great example to others who'd noticed him. If there ever was one card in the history of the game that summed up a player in a photograph, then this one was it for me. He's not standing there with a bat in his hands or squatting in the catcher's position. And it's not just a Thurman Munson action shot— it's a Thurman Munson *reaction* shot, one we've seen so many times during his career. It probably should be shown and used by managers at every level of the game, shown at team meetings or individual meetings because there'd be no reason for words. It's been said that a picture paints a thousand words. Just passing this card around and saying nothing would be sufficient in making a point.

Chapter 4
The Numbers Come to Life

"I looked out at left field after dusting myself off at third base, and Scott Livingston was smiling and nodding... that was enough for me."

If I could place an asterisk above a year of firsts in my young life, 1971 would be that year for any number of reasons.

1971 would be the first time I'd attended a major league game, it would be my first of many visits to the National Baseball Hall of Fame in Cooperstown and while Thurman Munson making his first all-star team in 1971 may not have been something personal, well, for me, it felt like it was.

The first major league baseball game I attended was at Shea Stadium when I was still wheelchair bound.

My moms cousin, Billy Burke, got us tickets to a Mets game but I wasn't told that at first. My dad just loaded me in the car like he always did and said he was taking me to see the Mets. To say I was excited had to be the biggest understatement of the year. Of course I would have preferred going to see the Yankees and Thurman at Yankee Stadium, but this was a big deal for me. My first major league game in person!

When they carried me in and I saw that field for the first time, it was so beautiful, it was like nothing else I'd ever seen before, not even close to any Little League field or even what I'd imagine one to look like. This was a full-scale major league park, not a little 12 inch image from our black and white TV, or any photos or drawings from magazines or the newspaper. I'd even taken notice to the size and scale of the parking lot, so many parked cars and cars parking and fans moving towards the gate.

And when we weaved our way towards our lower-level seats, I couldn't believe how green the grass was, the sheer size of the place, its perfect rows with thousands of seats, each deck a different color. Yellow, brown, blue and green seats made it look like a painting, and even the foul poles were painted a distinct orange.

Some people were in their seats and others were milling around or standing in concession lines. Vendors were barking out whatever they had for sale— programs, scorecards, hot dogs, peanuts— all of it. An organist was playing some catchy tunes, and later when the game started one fan I remembered seeing on TV when the Mets won the World Series was holding up large signs with sayings he'd thought of, looking for— and getting— reactions from the crowd, and I spotted some huge cameras around the park and wondered if they were the ones the used for their television broadcasts.

I was wearing a bright red sweatshirt and sitting in a box seat with my dad on the lower level when one of those cameras zoomed in on me. It wasn't until later when we got back home I learned my mom was watching the game at home and saw me on TV. She screamed so loud, our neighbor, Mr. Donachie, came running over from across the street and thought something was wrong. But my mother screamed, "Tommy was just on Television!"

I had no idea all this collaboration went on behind the scenes of a baseball game. It was so orchestrated and busy with so many moving parts. Everything that went into pre-game and even during the game drew me even closer to the game. It felt like watching movie previews at the theatre prior to the actual showing of the movie, something to get your interest before the main event.

About halfway through the game I remember listening when they announced the paid attendance. I don't recall what that number was, but knowing what the seating capacity was and seeing the number of fans and empty seats, it gave me a better perspective. I know I was only eight years old, but I'd already been reading boxscores and the attendance figure was always posted at the bottom.

I started to pay attention to that kind of thing after that—the attendance figures, time of the game—even who the umpires were that day. I'd look at every boxscore from every team and noticed that the Mets home attendance figures usually had topped that of most teams, and almost always was way better than that of the Yankees.

It had been less than two years since the Mets won the 1969 World Series and they were still the toast of the town, and Shea Stadium was still considered a new ballpark. I hadn't learned yet that the National League Los Angeles Dodgers and the San Francsico Giants both had teams in New York, and when they left town not that long ago some of that big hole in the hearts of New York and Brooklyn baseball fans was filled in by the Mets. There was a lot to be learned.

By the end of that 1971 season, the Mets had doubled the attendance figures of the Yankees and I still found that hard to believe. I didn't know that attendance was usually predicated on being a winning team—especially one challenging for a pennant. While the Mets had been in first place or close to it into June, the Yankees got off to a bad start and never challenged and finished a distant fourth place.

Before I even looked at the boxscores of what each player did that day, I scrolled down to the bottom to check out the attendance figures. I noticed the Mets had been drawing crowds of 40,000 or more into August and the Yankees had only one crowd over 20,000 the whole month of September, and some games there were just three or four thousand in the stands. That really bothered me for some reason.

It bothered me because so many thousands of fans were going to see the Mets, but they didn't have Thurman Munson, or Bobby Murcer or Roy White to see and they certainly didn't have a Yankee Stadium to see. Of course I was too young to understand any traffic problems around Yankee Stadium and other logistics issues, but it just didn't add up to me. By seasons end, I began to understand from listening to my brothers and following the standings that the Yankees had no chance reaching the post-season. It was probably sometime in August when I really started following the standings in both leagues and took notice to the records of just the Yankees and the Mets. In my young mind I pretended it was sort of a World

Series between the teams— a regular season World Series in which the team with the best record at the end of the year was going to be the champion of baseball.

Of course I was watching as many games as I could on WPIX. And if my brothers or my dad was watching the game with me, I'd ask them every now and then to switch over to WOR to see how the Mets were doing. And even though I rooted for the Mets in 1969, I couldn't now. My allegiance was to the Yankees, and when they had a west coast trip in mid-August the games were on way past my bedtime. I'd go to bed and think about that game and would align the Yankees in their usual positions and batting order: *Horace Clarke- second base... Thurman Munson- catcher... Bobby Murcer-center field... Roy White-left field...* I'd see each of them in the field, at the plate, in the dugout and I'd go to sleep thinking about the game and couldn't wait to get up to find out who won.

I mostly concentrated on Thurman Munson and wished great things for him those nights— I always wished for that. But not being able to see him on late night Yankee games I felt that whatever I hoped for—whatever I wished for him— would happen. That I had some sort of magical powers that would somehow transfer from me to him and he'd lead the Yankees to victory.

I equated having a good game with how many hits he'd have, and knew that having two or more was a very good game— something he did a lot of. And if he had one hit or no hits, I knew he'd bounce back the next game because he was that kind of player.

So I followed those Mets-Yankees standings right down to the wire and down to the wire it went. Not once from when I started to follow both teams records in August had the Yankees led the Mets, but they kept chipping away. And with one game left in the season they'd pulled to with one game.

The Mets would be at home against the Cardinals, but they had Tom Seaver on the mound. He had already won 20 games, and I knew that winning 20 games for a pitcher was like batting .300 for a hitter. The Yankees would be in Washington— the last game before the Senators would be moving to Texas for the 1972 season.

I knew there was a possibility the teams could end up with the exact same records, and knew that they wouldn't play each other to break that tie— but there was an easy fix to my dilemma— The Mayor's Trophy Game—an annual game between and Yankees and Mets that determined New York superiority—and the Yankees had won that game 2-1.

The Yankees did their part winning a game forfeited in the last inning when unruly fans stormed the field and began vandalizing it. I had no concept what any of that was, why fans would wreck their own ballpark like that. I'd seen riots and clashes on the news but couldn't equate any of that with baseball. Baseball was pure joy to me- a beautiful game surrounded by so much entertainment. I was confused by what happened in Washington.

But my scenario never worked out. Seaver won easily, and the Mets edged out the Yankees by one game. It was mind games like this one and others that really helped me better understand baseball. I'm not saying I understood all the numbers or knew how to calculate percentages or even how they were arrived at because I didn't. All I'm saying is I was getting *hooked* on numbers and had a simple understanding of what a good team record was and knew what a good batting average was, things like that. Following the standings and reading the boxscores and the listing of all players statistics in the Sunday paper was a big deal for me— a precursor of things to come. I was way ahead of my peers when it came to math and always enjoyed solving numbers problems, and baseball statistics was no exception.

I gave my mind a rest when we vacationed throughout upstate, New York that summer. Howe Caverns, the Catskills and a trip to Cooperstown. I enjoyed the caverns and the Catskills but what I really wanted to see was the Hall of Fame in Cooperstown.

I wasn't sure what to expect when we arrived, but it felt like home to me. There were no tall buildings or busy streets or traffic problems to contend with. Just an ordinary street filled with families, groups, couples, singles—all walking around, coming in and out of the many stores and the Hall of Fame.

There seemed to be a hundred rooms in the building but I was focused on seeking as many Yankee items or plaques that I could—particularly those of Babe Ruth.

Babe Ruth was one of those names I'd first heard from Phil Rizzuto on Yankee telecasts that really pulled me into becoming a Yankee fan- a diehard Yankee fan. Babe Ruth seemed bigger than life to me, almost fictitious like Casey At The Bat. I'd heard so many Babe Ruth stories and now that I had a better understanding of how many home runs made for a good season, I couldn't believe how many he'd hit and that I was in the same building where his uniform, his glove and even his locker were displayed.

My brothers had told me there was a special Babe Ruth phone at the Museum where you could have a conversation with Babe and I remember making that call to him, wondering how it could possibly be that I was talking with Babe Ruth, and he'd been dead for nearly a quarter century. It was one of those magical moments, believing in something that just couldn't be possible, but there I was, picking up the phone and hearing Babe Ruth's voice on the other end. And despite having such a vivid memory of my youth, I don't recall anything he may have said or if I said anything back to him. I was probably too frozen and too awestruck to have said a word.

But I could easily picture Babe Ruth hitting one into the right field stands at Yankee Stadium because I'd watched, *The Babe Ruth Story* on TV that year. I'd simply close my eyes and picture him circling the bases with those tiny steps he took, almost dancing his way to home plate while taking his time and tipping his cap and waving to the crowd. I remember his barrel chest and skinny legs that looked like they belonged to another person—almost like a caricature—and I thought, "He did that 714 times!"

I think that was the first time I was in total awe of someone because I wasn't seeing part of their life on TV or from afar, I was seeing it in person and hearing a voice in person—one I took as real. I stood in front of baseball treasures—artifacts just inches away from me that set my mind into motion inside that baseball world of mine. I was just enamored with Cooperstown and my entire baseball journey. It was a special feeling I had that day in Cooperstown and one I still have whenever I go back.

That same 1971 season, Thurman Munson made his first all-star team, and I was beside myself. I'd learned about the Rookie Of The Year Award after Thurman won it in 1970, and making an all-star team seemed so natural for him after that, and now that he'd become an all-star, I just knew it would be the first of many.

We watched the all-star games back then with all the fervor of watching or listening to the World Series. It was a big deal and gave us the chance to see all the greats from both leagues and that 1971 all-star game will go down in history with a mind-boggling 19 future Hall of Famers from both rosters.

By the end of that summer I'd finished my second year of home-schooling and was just weeks away from transitioning from wheelchair to crutches. I knew I was making good progress, because that's what Dr. Trinkle told me at every appointment. I'd gotten so used to hearing him tell me that, so I wasn't really prepared the day he told me I was ready to rise out of my chair into the final stage— the crutches. You can imagine the thrill on my face when I looked at him and wondered if I'd heard him right. I don't recall any celebrating of that event. Sure, it was a major step in the journey but I still had a long ways to go and now had to learn how to use crutches.

When I went from the chair to the crutches it was hard trying to get the hang of it. I'd been off my feet for two years and remember falling several times in the house my first night on them. It was hilarious! I laughed so hard each and every time I fell. I couldn't believe how wobbly my kegs were and why I couldn't control my mind into making them work. My legs felt like they were asleep and I kept going down. But I was in my glory. I was out of that wheelchair.

I kept at it and after only a few nights of struggling it was full speed ahead. My parents and siblings were afraid I'd get hurt but I had no such concerns. I could go to the bathroom by myself, move around while standing up and be so much more self-sufficient. I started becoming very brave on crutches and even started to get away with taking things a bit far at times.

I was outside playing on my crutches one day and despite the hinderance could really move fast. We were playing kickball, having a great time when my dad noticed me and yelled, "Tommy, get in here. You can't be running on that leg!" I told him I wasn't, but he didn't believe me and pulled me in off the street with all the kids watching. He insisted I was using that leg and I kept telling him I wasn't. And my brother yelled once at me because he thought I was kneeling, I never did any of that, either. Everyone knew they were responsible for me and they tended to go overboard sometimes.

The beautiful thing was I was back in school with my friends in the third grade, so there was plenty of time during recess to take it to another level, knowing I wasn't being watched too closely.

One day during recess, I was rumbling with my friend Tommy Paris and a few others when someone broke one of my crutches. All of us just stared at it for a few seconds and knew we'd get in trouble unless we told a fib. When we went back to class I pretended to walk across the room and break it. I said, "Oh no, my crutch just broke"! Our teacher, Mrs. Smith said, "Tom Tunison... you didn't just break your crutch, did you?" I said Yes, I did," and she asked "How did you break it, because I didn't hear it snap." I had to tell her the truth about it. So the next three of four months I went around on one crutch! I don't remember the outcome and don't remember what happened when I got home, but I probably was punished.

They never did replace that broken crutch, and even after all these years later I don't know why. All I can figure is that my left leg had healed enough, and all I needed from that point forward was a crutch for my right side.

By 1972 I was old enough to try out for the Little League Minors. I had watched my brothers play Little League ball and watched Thurman Munson and the Yankees on TV, and longed to get out on a field myself. I was still on one crutch and wasn't sure if I'd be allowed to tryout, but when they announced that I could, I was ecstatic.

I'd already adapted quite well to walking with just one crutch, then transitioned into partially playing in any kickball games or wiffle-ball games that sprung up in the neighborhood. I'd kick the ball with my opposite leg or stand in the batters box and bang out a wiffle-ball, and while I stood there wanting so badly to run the bases, I remember them saying, "Who's running for Tommy,?" and a chorus of eager voices would answer, "I'll run for him!"

I was happy that at least I was participating, but being young and adventurous— and perhaps foolish— I started running them out with that crutch tucked under my arm.

I'd always been a fast runner and still was, crutch and all. There was no pain or swelling or even a cramp when I ran, and at times when I'd rub my bad leg it felt as good as my good leg did. I knew it was only a matter of when they'd be telling me I'd be free from that crutch for good, but for now, I'd have to handle the upcoming tryout with it.

It didn't really bother me that I'd be trying out that way. I wasn't really self-conscious about it because everyone I knew had gotten used to seeing me that way. All I knew was that I was going to play Little League baseball with umpires and uniforms and white bases with foul lines. There'd be fences and people on the bleachers and even a scoreboard. Man... this was big time for me.

I knew from my brothers that tryouts would be in front of all the coaches from the league and when it ended, one of them would draft you and notify you that night. They told me it was a nervous moment in time when all eyes are on just you as they hit you grounders, fly balls and line-drives to see how you'd field, throw and move around. I imagined all they'd told me and was anxious to show them what I could do.

I still wasn't allowed to walk on that right leg during tryouts, but I'd learned to shift any ball that came to me over to my throwing hand by flipping my glove, taking the ball out, tucking the glove back under may arm and throwing the ball wherever it needed to go—just like Jim Abbot did in later years.

I'll never forget how quiet it was when I went out to the middle of the gym all by myself with my crutch and glove. I could hear the whispering and I could feel them watching me as I fielded grounders and popups, so confidently firing it back in. Now the whispers had turned to statements regarding my arm, things being said about me like, "Look at that arm!" or, "That's amazing!" It was just an unbelievable and unforgettable feeling for me and a dream come true. Later that night, the coach for the Bears called me and said, "Tommy. I picked you. You're a Bear."

It was a hard feeling to put into words. Three years of being so isolated and so longing to play again was something nobody else could really understand. I didn't really think of it then, but now I know how that period in my life really helped mold me into someone who never quits, someone who understands what it takes to follow a dream and to be grateful for every bit of it. It has helped me to be thankful, that this is what God has done for me, these three stages of trials leading to a freedom that can't be described. And just a few days later with my friend Eddie Short by my side, and before the start of the season, Dr. Trinkle told me it was completely over— I'd healed beautifully and wouldn't need that last crutch again.

You can imagine the thrill on my face when I looked at him and wondered if I'd heard him right. And he said it again, "You're all better. You did a great job."

So I asked him if I could play football and he said no, that he wanted me to promise that I'd never play football. Then I asked him if I could play baseball, and he said I could play all the baseball I wanted to. That was music to my ears.

The timing couldn't have been better as we took the field a few days later for my first Minor League Little League game. It was quite a day for me as you could well imagine, and with my mother and sister Ginnie attending, I was happy they were there and hopeful for something good to happen, something memorable that we could take home and share with the rest of the family. I don't recall being nervous or scared, but was rather anxious to get on the field and to get my first at bat.

My mom rarely went to any more games after that. Not because she wasn't interested or didn't want to, it was all because of family— the other six kids at home always needing guidance and care that prevented her from being there. But while I was home watching the Yankees on TV, mom sat with me and shared that same passion I had for the Yankees, rooting and cheering and bonding with me.

My friend, Scott Livingston, was playing left field for the other team and knew I'd be batting for the first time soon, so when we crossed paths on the field he dared me to hit one over his head when I came up. Of course I took that as a great challenge and kept his words close to the vest until the moment I came to the plate.

Well, the bases were loaded when I came to bat— something I'd envisioned a million times already. I think most kids my age that loved and followed baseball like I did had that same image in their mind from time to time, coming up with the bases loaded and hitting a grand-slam to win the game. Its sort of a right of passage, I think, to imagine that happening to you, and now *it was* happening to me in my very first at bat.

I wanted nothing more than to cream one over the head of Scott Livingston in left field, to make him eat his words and think twice about daring me again. And I wanted to show myself and my mother and sister what I was made of.

When I arrived at third base after clearing the bases with a long triple over the head of Scott Livingston in left field, everybody was cheering for me, not so much for that triple, but for just being on that field again. Everybody knew my story and I'm sure it was a feel-good moment for those who saw it that day. What they didn't know stayed between me and Scott Livingston.

I looked out at left field after dusting myself off at third base, and Scott Livingston was smiling and nodding... that was enough for me.

Chapter 5
Ecstasy & Agony

"I was becoming a different fan now—a student of the game- watching the game with a different set of eyes..."

When we weren't playing organized Little League games, just about everything else we did centered around baseball. We played with hollow, super-pinkies that bounced like a super-ball, reaching heights as high as 30 feet with a good, hard throw against the pavement. We played stickball with a broomstick and could hit one of those pinkies the proverbial mile. Sometimes a ball would roll down the street too fast and too far away and would find its way into a sewer opening before we could run it down, forcing us to switch to another game with a different type of ball. Any ball we'd get our hands on we'd invent some improvised game of baseball.

There were a few times when I'd find myself alone, but I'd learned to be creative, and had been since the days I was bed-ridden in my body cast, throwing that little rubber ball in the air all day long. It helped me become independent on those few times when friends weren't around, and in was something I actually looked forward to. I enjoyed that challenge of using my mind, to take a good look around me and size up what was available to invent some new game. I could easily envision a baseball field by any number of things, be it the trees, the street or even a wall. In fact, I fastened a string onto our chain-link fence in the shape of the strike zone that was 45 feet away— Little League pitching distance—and would throw a wiffle ball against it over and again— for a complete nine-inning game. It was tedious retrieving each pitch I threw but that didn't bother me. I was lost inside my baseball world and that was all that mattered.

I think the wiffle-ball probably really did it for me as far as wanting to be a pitcher. I didn't have very big hands to be able to throw a good curveball and never really developed one in later years, but because of the wiffle-ball I learned to throw a Ron Guidry-type slider and even a Carl Hubbell-like screwball by junior high school and became a very effective-pitcher with an assortment of pitches that could fool a batter. I really wanted to be a pitcher.

After just one season with the Bears, coach Dave Teason chose me to play for the Major League Indians. Just hearing or seeing the words, *Major League* always reminded me of going pro— that I'd made it as far as I could for now— a big leaguer, just like Thurman Munson was. We had a young team that year with mostly 10 and 11 year-olds, and for anyone remembering being on a young Little League team, that usually meant a long season with few victories and that team was no exception. Our only victory was achieved around the mid point of the season when coach Teason penciled me in to pitch against—of all teams— the Yankees and my friend Charlie Summers.

We hadn't really been in many close games to that point, and trailed, 4-2 going into bottom of the sixth. That's when our catcher, Doug Vernet hit one off the top of the fence to clear the bases for the victory—walk off style.

You would have thought we'd just won the World Series after the winning run crossed home plate, it felt that good—and I was the winning pitcher. We both got game balls after that, and later when I replayed that game over and over in my mind, I fell asleep with it on the couch, that game ball resting on my chest.

There's something to be said when you play for a team winning just one game an entire season. It can be a bit embarrassing and certainly frustrating with the constant beatings most every game, but there's no doubt it makes you appreciate when a championship season happens— and they are few when they do happen— that brings a humility that never goes away, an appreciation for the journey. In years that followed, I'd come to know that feeling all too well.

I was pitching in the championship game a few years later when I was 12—and remains as one of the most memorable games of my life. Not only was it a big deal for me, but we were going up against the Reds— the same Reds coached by my father's boss, Mr. Firestone.

I remember pitching and beating them earlier in that same season, striking out 12 batters in a 4-2 win. My father was so happy, I gave him the game ball they gave to me and he took it to work with him the next day— happy we'd won against his boss's team.

We were winning the championship game 10-3 with only two innings to go when things started falling apart. They scored six runs in the bottom of the fifth and when I finally recorded the last out of the inning I was petrified— a feeling I'd never felt before— almost too afraid to go on.

We picked up a run in the sixth, but because of what happened in the fifth, I had lost my confidence and was a mess. I stopped striking out batters like I was used to doing all season, and we when we stopped making the plays in the field, it affected me.

It didn't talk long for the Reds to put men on base, so Coach Teason came out the mound to try and pick me up. He said, "Tommy... you're the best in the league... there's nobody better. You've done it before and you can do it again... now shut them down."

But I didn't shut them down... we lost, 12-11.

I was balling my eyes out as the winning run scored, and I wanted to hide inside myself and shut out the rest of the world. But I mustered up the courage to walk off that mound to make that long walk back to my dugout, trying hard to hold back the tears that ran down my cheeks. The Reds players even sensed what I was feeling and came over to our dugout to try and console me, but I was devastated.

When we held that 10-3 lead, all I was thinking was there would be no way we could blow such a big lead, and began thinking about the baseball trophies my brothers had earned being on winning teams. I could see myself holding my own trophy now— my very first trophy— holding it proudly and even taking it to bed with me that night. To go from certain victory to an empty pit was the most horrible feeling I'd ever had.

I'd heard the phrase, "Ecstasy of winning and agony of defeat," and I knew what that meant. And while it took some time to try and get that awful loss and sinking feeling out of my mind, it never went away.

It would take another two years for me to have another shot at earning my first trophy in baseball—a tense, nail-biting three game series of our "Senior" Little League finals.

I had gone from Bears to Indians to Matadors, and now my good buddy, Matt Manzella was a teammate of mine, and another good friend, Craig Stapleton played for our opponent in that final series.

Craig and I would later become teammates in the seventh grade— battery-mates actually (Craig's a prominent figure later in the book) and he'd established himself as quite a catcher already— sort of cut from the Thurman Munson catcher's mold. He was tough as nails and was all about winning and we were friends outside the lines. But this was serious business— all business for now. After I won the first game on the mound and we lost the second game, that set up the one game winner take-all-final.

I was on second base late in the game with two outs and our team holding a 6-3 lead. A feeling came over me just then that I had to run as fast as I could wherever the next ball was going to be hit. The image of a routine fly ball being hit to the infield came to me just then and when our batter hit a looping fly ball towards their shortstop, I said to myself, "Run with all you've got, Tom!" I headed for third like I was running the hundred yard dash, took the corner and headed home. I looked over my shoulder as the ball came down, that routine fly now popping out of the glove of their shortstop.

"I knew it!" I said to myself as I crossed the plate.

We took that 7-3 lead into their last at bat, but they chipped away and cut our lead to 7-6, two outs and the bases loaded. I was playing shortstop, Matt was at second and Craig was the baserunner on first when a high chopper was hit my way.

It seemed like an eternity for that ball to come down and I could hear Craig steaming towards the bag at second. When the ball finally landed in my glove, I kept my cool, watched Craig begin his slide then flipped the ball to Matt covering second, just in time to record the final out of the game. Like two choreographed dancers, we leaped into the air together. It was my first trophy.

By then, I really started paying attention to the efforts being made by a teams battery—its pitcher and catcher—particularly the concentration and stamina needed by the pitcher, and a warrior-like mentality from its catchers and to a number of premonitions like the one I had during that championship game.

I had already developed strong shoulders and arms by then, mostly from hopping around on my crutches for an entire year. With additional years of tossing and throwing balls at every waking moment, I'd developed a stamina to go the distance on the mound, showing no signs of fatigue or losing any velocity off my fastball.

And sure, I'd watched Thurman Munson behind the plate during Yankee telecasts, but to witness first hand what a catcher goes through game after game when Doug Vernet was my teammate enlightened me. How he managed his position with balls bouncing off his chest-protector, his shin-guards and taking foul balls off his mask certainly opened my eyes to what a catcher does through every game.

While we were fighting for wins, the Yankees were fighting for respectability, their 1972 season another such year for the Yankees and for Thurman Munson. That the Yankees finished fourth wasn't the entire story of their season, and that Thurman was passed over for the all-star team was another. Even into mid-September they'd pulled to within a half game of the lead then fell apart down the stretch. Of course I was riveted to every game at that time, and loved the feeling of having my team in a pennant race that late in the season.

But the Yanks lost their last five games of the year— an agonizing and helpless feeling as Boston and Detroit battled down to the wire— with the Tigers winning by a weird half game difference.

There had been a players strike that altered the regular season into an unbalanced schedule, and that's what cost the Red Sox in the end. Even then I had developed a sense of fairness and even though I was a true-blue Yankee fan, this one bothered me. It just didn't seem fair to have something like that happen to any team, to play all those games and to then lose out like they did. I really wondered how a decision like that had been made and approved of by the powers in charge.

But while serious Yankee fans were greatly disappointed in the Yankees late season collapse, some seemed even happier with what happened to the Red Sox and is when I began to learn more about the Yankees-Red Sox rivalry.

Of course I had no way of knowing what the future held in store for both players, or for what was coming down the pike between the teams, but in a sense, it was that 1972 all-star game snub of Thurman that began my passion for not only following Thurman and Carlton Fisk, but for following and understanding the catching position in general.

That following 1973 season when both Munson and Fisk made the American League all-star team, I watched the game like I always had, but found myself rooting somewhat differently than I had before. Sure, I was happy Thurman made the team but didn't understand why Fisk was chosen as its starter. I was an American League fan and always rooted for them to win that game, but when Fisk came up to bat I found myself torn.

• • •

It's not like I was rooting against Carlton Fisk, but when I looked at the boxscores every day I always wanted Thurman to do better than him, and now that they were teammates it made for some deep-soul-searching.

Fisk hit a couple of decent shots to the outfield in his two at bats, both caught by the outfielders, but was still in the game after five innings. I was hoping this wouldn't be a repeat of Thurmans's first all-star game from 1971 when he never even got into the game, and finally in the sixth, I took a sigh of relief when Thurman went in for Fisk.

Of course I was disappointed when Thurman popped weekly to first in the seventh and struck out in the ninth, but he was being talked about by the announcers in the same conversation with Fisk and the National League's Johnny Bench and Ted Simmons, that there was about to be a changing of the guard in that position— a position of dominance held by the Tigers Bill Freehan since 1963.

I pulled out my Bill Freehan baseball card at some point during that game and marveled that he'd been chosen as an American League all-star for the tenth straight season. And as I studied his statistics and mulled a few things over, I took notice to three things I hadn't really paid attention to before—games played, hits per season and players age.

I'd noticed a sudden drop-off in Freehan's games played in 1970, then up again in 1971 then back down in 72. I didn't recall knowing if he'd been injured during those seasons, but I had no idea how to find that out. All I knew was that he'd produced under 100 hits during those two down years, and he was now in his early 30's. Nevertheless, I was intrigued as to why Freehan had missed so many games.

I ran for my box of baseball cards and sorted out all the catcher's cards I had in my collection. I didn't have them all but I charted those I had, referencing the 1972 season, noting games played, hits produced and their ages. That's when I decided to key in on *Games Played* for some reason.

Thurman had played 140 games that season, so I started there, searching my baseball cards for any catcher at, above or below that line. I was eager to find out if any one American League player had played more games than Thurman, and hoping beyond hope that no one had. As I neared the end of that search, I noted only a few players had been in over 120 games and only three— Ray Fosse (134), Dick Billings (133) and Fisk (131)— passed the 130 mark.

It was far from being perfect or even close to being completely accurate, but it satisfied me to a point. It came to mind that the back of a baseball card didn't tell the whole story about games played, and I'd noticed in the boxscores that many of the players I'd just researched played at multiple positions on he field. Accurate or not, that *games played* number was telling me something, telling a story inside the actual statistics of a player, telling me something about durability and that Thurman Munson was at the top.

It really irked me that the announcers referenced Bench and Fisk and Simmons more often as the catching barometers of baseball, that Thurman wasn't given his due, that he was sort of like the step-sister of that catching quartet. And even though I hadn't yet looked at my National League baseball cards to see how many game Bench and Simmons and all the rest of them played, I wondered if the announcers knew what I knew about

Thurman and if so, why hadn't they mentioned anything about the durability factor during that telecast.

At the end of that 1973 season, Boston once again finished ahead of the Yankees in the standings, but fell short once again of making the post-season since an improbable 1967 season when they lost to the Cardinals in the World Series. But the Red Sox had inched closer to the top of the standings than the Yankees had and that concerned me. I wondered if Thurman Munson would ever experience what it felt like to be in the World Series, or how I'd feel if that happened.

I had changed my way of thinking about baseball into another level. No longer was I just a casual fan watching the games for fun and checking the boxscores. I'd become a student of the game, watching and studying with a different set of eyes, charting rarely used statistics, and developing a baseball maturity miles removed from that wide-eyed boy from a few years ago.

Chapter 6
Winthrop Avenue

"I learned especially from my brother, Roy, things that spoke volumes about him and would have a profound affect on me in later years."

By 1974, the Yankees had started changing the make-up of their team, due in part to their impatient and sometimes petulant new owner George Steinbrenner.

Steinbrenner had taken over the reigns a year earlier and made a lasting statement on opening day, enforcing a military-style grooming code forbidding most facial hair not be grown below the collar— and Thurman Munson was among those he singled out.

I didn't give much thought to these types of things and don't remember giving it much thought at the time. I just didn't like that Thurman was grouped with others in sort of a negative light, and knew that Thurman was opinionated and probably wouldn't like it. I was more interested in knowing the scores from games, the league standings, what we needed to do to get better, that sort of thing. The politics of the game I largely ignored. I think it at all blew over in time, but the New York press had their day with it. But that Yankee season—that Yankee season— was a roller coaster ride like none other since the days I started following them.

For the first month of the season, the Yanks toyed with first place, and by months end were tied with Baltimore for first place in a very cramped American League East Division. By June 1st they'd slipped to fourth, a month later into last place and by August 1st climbed out of the cellar by a half game over the Tigers.

There wasn't much talk about the Yankees getting back into the race. With two months to go, playing under .500 ball, having to leap over so many teams in front of them and losing seven of their last eight games, it just didn't seem likely that they'd make their move. That's when Thurman got hot.

Thurman was definitely having an off year, but he'd injured his hand during spring training and wasn't the same player. But he didn't miss any games, played through the pain and during that Yankees August push he clubbed four homers, knocked in 23 and batted .326, carrying the Yankees to an 18-10 record that pulled the club to within two games of Boston with 30 to go.

It had been the first time in decades that both the Yankees and Red Sox had been relevant at the same time at such a late juncture of the season, a three team race bunched up with Baltimore into the closing weeks of the season. As the Yankees played into the pennant race, Rizzuto started mentioning the 1949, down-to-the-wire race against the Red Sox, sharing bits and pieces from that seasons final games, building to a climatic final two game series against Boston, trailing by one game in the standings.

They'd packed Yankee Stadium for those final two games with Boston, and when they rallied from a 4-0 deficit in that first game to win 5-4, it was as if Phil was back on that field again, and I was in the stands cheering for him, for an aging Joe DiMaggio and an up and coming catcher named Yogi Berra. And then when they won it the next day in front of nearly 70,000 fans, I'd learned some new Yankee names like Jerry Coleman, Cliff Mapes, Vic Raschi and others, categorizing each name in my head and eager to learn more about them at some point later on.

Rizzuto had talked about the unbelievable second half of the season by the Red Sox, overcoming a 12 game deficit to the Yankees, sweeping the Yankees at Fenway just a few days earlier in a three game series and surging into the lead for the first time all year. With four games to go Phil mentioned that he and everybody else knew it was coming down to those final two games at home.

I had no trouble visualizing any of what Phil was saying. It was as if he'd been broadcasting any part of those games on the radio, and I'd close my eyes and put everything into place and could see everything as clear as the day I went to Shea Stadium for the first time. I'd put it all to mind and with a monumental comeback by the Yankees dancing in my head, I truly believed the Yankees would stay hot and win the darn thing.

There'd been talk in New York comparing the 1973 Mets with these Yankees— a season ending with the Mets posting the worst won-lost record (82-79) for any team making the post-season in the history of the game, then losing to Oakland in the World Series.

I'd kept my daily habit of checking the boxscores and the attendance figures and couldn't for the life of me understand why the Mets were still outdrawing the Yankees. The Mets had taken a big free fall in the standings and would finish 20 games under .500, and despite the fact that both teams were playing home games at Shea Stadium during the renovation of Yankee Stadium, the Mets still were winners at the box office—something that always seemed to annoy me.

I still remember when Baltimore came into town for a three game series, trailing the Yankees by two and a half games with 14 to play and needing to sweep the Yankees to knock them out of first place. It was unthinkable that the Orioles would win all three, or to even take one game, but when they won game one, then game two and the series final game, the unthinkable had happened. Even with the Yanks winning their last five games of the year, they couldn't catch the red-hot Orioles who reeled off a nine game winning streak to close out the season.

If anything, I got a sense of what a rivalry can be and learned that for rivalries to really heat up, both teams needed to be challenging for the pennant at the same time, starting with pre-season predictions or from what may have happened the previous year. In a strange way the ending to that 1974 season circled me back to the game I lost against the Reds, how I blew a 10-3 lead late in the game, and that terrible, gut-wrenching feeling that followed. It felt no different now.

The Yankees had come ever so close to winning it, and now had the entire winter to think about it, to mull over some of their tough losses like I was doing, checking off games they'd blown and should have won. I had a hunch Thurman Munson was probably back home, shouldering the blame and wondering what more he could have done.

That winter off-season became a whirlwind of player movement for the Yankees that began at the end of the World Series and right into spring training of 1975.

The Yankees traded or released guys like Bill Sudakis and Sam McDowell, and had already dealt or released other known names like Lindy McDaniel, Horace Clarke, Hal Lanier and Ron Swoboda over the past two seasons. And looking back on that Yankee team of 1973 it seemed to me they had a roster full of aging veterans—guys who'd been all-stars or key players before but now had passed their prime playing years, guys like Johnny Callison, Bernie Allen and Duke Sims. And I recall looking at that Yankee roster and noting how many ex-San Francisco Giant players they had, like Felipe and Matty Alou, Jim Ray Hart and Hal Lanier, and wondered how and why that was. Whatever it was it wasn't over. I was at Scott Livingston's house when we heard that the Yankees had traded Bobby Murcer to the Giants for slugger Bobby Bonds. We took a double-take at each other then listened some more.

We were big Bobby Murcer fans and like most of us at the time, we were shocked at the trade. Even though he started out playing third base for the Yankees, Bobby had followed in the center field footsteps of Joe DiMaggio and Mickey Mantle, heading for stardom and undoubtedly would be a Yankee for life. He'd made his fourth straight all-star team, and despite his home run production slipping, he was still knocking in runs with the best of them and I knew— I just knew—that moving to Shea Stadium during that year while Yankee Stadium underwent a remodel was the difference in his home run production, that so many of his home runs at Yankee Stadium landed beyond the short right field porch and that he'd be back doing it again in another year.

I found it hard to believe the Yankees had given up on Bobby like that. He'd hit a third of the Yankees home runs in 1972, and like Thurman, he rarely missed a game. Sure, Bobby Bonds was going to be a nice addition, but what I'd learned from Rizzuto about Yankee tradition and loyalty seemed to be forgotten now.

I think the expectations for Bobby Murcer contributed to that trade, expectations of 40 home runs a year—like Mickey had done every year before. And as that realization set in that Bobby Murcer was going west, I wanted him to have his best year ever, to have a great career with the Giants, even to one day face the Yankees in the World Series. But beyond all that, I hoped even more that one day he'd be a Yankee again.

I had to welcome Bobby Bonds in as a Yankee, there was never a doubt in that. I'd learned enough about trades and players being released or retiring, and it wasn't Bobby Bonds fault for what had happened. I'd root for Bonds just like I rooted for any other Yankee before. And even though I rooted and cheered for Bobby Bonds with all my heart and soul, I found myself rooting and cheering and following Bobby Murcer with all my heart and soul as if he were still a Yankee.

It was only a few months later when the Yankees signed "Catfish" Hunter to a free agent contract— something new that was about to change the face of baseball. To that point I hadn't paid attention much to players contracts, all I knew was we had "Catfish" Hunter, and we were going to win the AL East that year, but my grand idea that the additions of Bonds and Hunter would put the Yankees over the top started falling apart right around the same time I attended my first Yankee game live on July 25th with my sister Debbie and her husband Heff. It had been less than a month when everything seemed to be going as planned. An 8-6 win at Fenway put the Yanks a half game up on the Sox and into first place— thanks in part to Thurman's bases loaded single that cleared the bases in the fifth.

That three hit game pushed Thurman's batting average over .340 for the season, and as I followed league standings religiously, I followed the daily listings of the top hitters in the league, wanting badly for Thurman to be number one in batting average. I scanned the boxscores from every game every single day, searching especially looking to see what Rod Carew of the Twins had done that day.

I'd known enough about Carew to know he'd be hard to overtake, and I was right. It seemed that every time Thurman got two hits, Carew would have three, and if Thurman had one hit, Carew would have two. Carew sure wasn't a power hitter, he just put the bat on the ball all the time and stroked it to wherever they weren't playing.

But as that batting race widened in Carew's favor, so did the league standings... in Boston's favor. Following that 8-6 win, the Yanks dropped 16 of their next 24 games and trailed the Sox by eight games on July 25th— the first live Yankee game of my life.

I'd always wanted to see the original Yankee Stadium for a home Yankee game, but its renovation wasn't completed. I'd attended a Mets game a few years earlier at Shea Stadium, and remembered everything about that experience, but I found out right away that the experience I had at Shea was not going to be duplicated this time.

From the time they'd announced before the game started that Thurman would be the designated hitter and Ed Hermann would be catching made me a bit angry. And the fact that Carlton Fisk— who just returned a few weeks earlier after being out for nearly three months— was catching for Boston, well, I didn't think that was fair, either. I had my heart set on watching Thurman Munson bat *and* play in the field, something I'd wanted and had looked forward to my entire, Yankee-watching life. It wasn't the same watching—ironically— that 8-6 Yankee win, but I cheered like crazy every time Thurman came to bat, and cheered even louder when he singled late in the game.

As that season unraveled for the Yankees and the Red Sox made it to the World Series, it bothered me a little that Carlton Fisk would be in the national spotlight and that Thurman would be back home watching the playoffs. Thurman ended up having a terrific season, winning his third straight Gold Glove, making his fourth all-star team, finished third in batting average behind Carew, finished fifth in runs batted in, seventh in the MVP voting and was even named AL Player of the Week in May.

By then I'd really taken notice to how many games Munson and Fisk had played in— something I'd charted since the all-star game from a few years back. Certainly Fisk was an important part of that Red Sox lineup, but the fact that over that two year period from 1974-75 he'd played in only 131 games to Thurman's 301 told me what

I wanted to know, that the durability factor was real and that the true value of a player to his team was in staying on the field.

For the life of me I couldn't understand why certain players got injured more than others, and why it was that Thurman wasn't heading that list. I'd watched enough games and seen enough plays at the plate where Thurman was knocked down, bowled over or totally annihilated, yet somehow was always able to hold onto the ball, pick himself up and get back to business. It just wasn't that way with everybody else.

When Fisk homered in game six of that classic series, "pushing" the ball towards fair territory with his hands, I felt a bit jealous. It was such a memorable moment that all of baseball and millions of fans watched on TV, but in my mind it was moments like that one that should have been reserved for Thurman Munson and the Yankees— not for Carlton Fisk or the Red Sox.

But it wasn't the Red Sox or Carlton Fisk that had me worried that winter, or even thinking about baseball for that matter. It was a decision I made during our Christmas break that almost cost me my life.

I was with my friends, Chris Pyatt, Keith Woodard, Phil Drago, Jerry Reynolds and Eddie Short when we decided to romp around town after dinner. It was raining as we made our way over to Winthrop Avenue elementary school, ready to be the daredevils we were. Winthrop had a series of roofs that we'd become very familiar with during any game we'd play that featured a ball. Often times we'd have to retrieve the many balls we'd hit or kick to the roof, be it a baseball, tennis ball or kick ball, climbing like monkeys would to the top of the canopy, totally unconcerned with falling, wanting only to retrieve that ball. Without a question all of us were thrill-seekers to the max, climbing anything, trees, buildings, you name it. There were times we'd climb some structure high enough and be able to see the New York City skyline and planes taking off from JFK airport— a very cool experience for adventuresome boys of 12.

There was a long awning above a steel flight of stairs at Winthrop that extended all the way to that third roof of the school. Being at its highest peak, it was possible—if you'd been brave enough or dumb enough— to climb to its awning, crawl your way to the very top then hoist yourself onto the roof where you'd be greeted by the most spectacular view you'd ever seen.

• • •

The rain had picked up a bit and being winter it made for slippery conditions. Despite my friends warnings not to do it, I started my climb, determined to reach the top. I don't know if being sidelined for three years that contributed to that decision to climb, and as I started telling then guys they were "chicken," I felt no fear as I started my climb.

I don't remember anything about falling after I reached the halfway point, only seeing my gloved hand as I reached for the wall of the school to take a breather.

From all accounts I fell like a rocket shot from a cannon, speeding towards the ground and picking up speed. When Keith tried desperately to catch me or even break my fall, I landed headfirst on the concrete, knocked unconscious with blood pouring from my nose and mouth, eyes rolling in my head.

The guys raced for a phone while someone else raced to my house just a quarter mile away. When my dad and my sister Lori arrived soon after, the rain had picked up and they crouched over me and held me, comforting me the best they could. While they waited for the ambulance to arrive, Lori heard me moaning about my arm, giving a narrow sense of relief to my friends who thought I was a goner.

I had never heard of any out-of-body experiences or seeing heaven at such times or anything remotely like that before, but I distinctly remember being high above the playground – and out of my body – seeing the swing sets around me then zooming back to earth like a rocket, watching my dad and sister kneeling over me. There was a certain peace in that moment of time, unearthly really. To this day I don't known if it was a Guardian Angel or God. But it was real. With no time for understanding any of what had happened to me, they placed me into the ambulance where EMT's assessed my injures and started treating me. One of them touched my face, and the pain was excruciating, setting off a chain-reaction of constant vomiting and spitting up blood. The next thing I remember was waking up in bed in a very large, bright room, totally alone, noticing the sun shining so radiantly into the room and realizing right then that I was alive. I felt totally at peace, an incredible feeling knowing that God had saved me and surprisingly was in no pain whatsoever.

I cocked my head slowly to my right and noticed that my right arm was in a cast. I wiggled my fingers sticking out of the cast, then cocked my head the other way, noticing my other arm connected to a bag on a free-standing hook. When I spotted its four wheels at the base, I pulled myself out of bed and headed straight for the bathroom, dragging my IV behind me.

I felt a terrible swelling over my right eye and wanted to see my face in the mirror, trying to imagine the extent of my injuries and preparing myself properly for what I was about to see. I looked into that mirror and didn't see myself at all, really surprised at what was looking back at me. I paused and kept looking at myself and despite massive swelling, my right eye completely red and being somewhat disfigured, I remember feeling grateful that I was alive and headed back to my hospital bed.

The glaring sun I'd witnessed just moments earlier had brightened to another level. I walked to the window and to my utter amazement the rain from the night before had turned to snow, altering the landscape from my 17th floor perch at Meadowbrook hospital into an endless paradise of the most perfect blanket of snow imaginable. It wasn't long after that when the doctor came and explained the injuries that occurred. My right arm – my throwing arm - fractured at the forearm and needing months to heal. My right cheekbone, broken above my right eye, "A miracle," he admitted, "that you survived that fall."

They monitored my progress for several days after that, checking on me around the clock. One afternoon when I was alone with the doctor he told me something that I wasn't ready for, that surgery was necessary to repair the damage to my head. I wasn't sure why he was telling me this, that my parents weren't there to comfort me and to ask adult questions. And when he left the room after dishing out that very matter-of-fact explanation to me, I became very upset.

My big brother Roy was a tough guy, a rough and tumble guy—the type of guy you wanted in your corner at all times. And as I thought about everything the Doctor just told me, Roy showed up in my room. He could tell I was distraught and wanted to know why and I told him. He calmed me down and told me he would be right back.

I found out later that Roy sought out the doctor and gave him a good tongue lashing when he found him. When my parents had finally been told some of what Roy and I already knew, they scheduled surgery on my eye orbit just days before Christmas. The thought of not being home in time for Christmas weighed heavily on my mind. Christmas at our house was amazing each year with so many presents under the tree and a family of nine gathered round. The nurses at the hospital understood, and they made a push for that operation to be performed sooner so I could be home for Christmas. It was that stand they took for me that made it happen, my surgery had been moved up a few days, and on Christmas Eve morning the doctor entered my room and said I would be heading home that night – pure joy!

My Dad arrived in late afternoon and we headed home, cast signed by all the nurses who made it happen. I couldn't wait to get home, to see the decorations around the house and the Christmas tree that always made me happy. But I felt a deeper appreciation this time as I walked through the door. The decorations and the trimmings on the tree seemed better and brighter than they had before. And we had an amazing celebration. I remember getting everything I had asked for that year, knowing I probably shouldn't have gotten a thing for the shenanigans I pulled, and felt so grateful and fortunate to even be alive.

You would have thought we learned our lesson from that fall from the roof, but we didn't. While my arm was still in a cast I was with my friends Eddie Short, Phil Drago and Jerry Reynolds spending an afternoon with Scott Livingston at his house. They lived on a canal that had frozen over when we decided to go out onto the frozen canal. Despite my arm being in that cast, I still managed to climb down a ladder with the rest of the guys and onto the dock that lead to the canal. One of the guys discovered that by jumping up and down the sound it made would result in a loud echo all the way down past the canal.

That wasn't good enough for our bunch. Someone decided that it might make a better sound if we jumped higher then off the dock onto what we thought was frozen-hard ice. I was quite the daredevil, and as much as I wanted to participate, I stayed put. When Eddie took his turn the ice gave way and into the frozen water he went.

Being with just one working arm, there was nothing I could do to help physically. I yelled at the guys to get him, but when Eddie resurfaced his frantic thrashing and grabbing at the ice made things worse, and the ice kept breaking away and the hole grew wider. But the guys kept their wits about them, formed a human chain and pulled Eddie to safety.

I learned a lot that year— a lot about friends and taking risks and about loyalty. I learned that friends would do whatever it takes for you, be it trying to break your fall or plunging into the ice to save your life, that despite all the risks and all the warnings, a true friend was always there. I learned that baseball loyalty was fleeting, despite what a player like Bobby Murcer had done for his team, and that a baseball family changed, like it or not, each and every year.

I learned especially from my brother Roy, things that spoke volumes about him and would have a profound affect on me in later years. That my 17 year old brother—unafraid and unwavering— would confront a doctor three times his age —demonstrated to me what loyalty was all about, that despite any family squabbles or problems we may have had, that he was there for me... for us... strong, capable and unnerved by nothing.

Chapter 7
Osgood-Schlatter

"I took it personally that Thurman's three hits, two walks and an RBI somehow came when I was in the stands, that the connection I'd felt with him was communicated in some spiritual way."

As the weeks went on the doctor designed a special guard to protect my head so that I could return to school for the 7th grade. It was an odd looking device, but it kept me safe and created lots of staring and comments being made. Being that I'd been bed-ridden, pushed around on a wheelchair and limping around on crutches for three years made me sort of immune to all that kind of attention, none of which bothered me.

My arm— my pitching arm— took quite a while to heal, but I wouldn't let that get me down or stop me from participating in some fashion. And, as I did when I tossed that little rubber ball into the air thousands of times when I was bed-ridden, I started throwing left-handed.

It took a while to get my brain and my left arm to work together, but I did it. The process went from me looking hilarious, on to improvement, then gaining control and finally mastering it. And while I never made the full transition to being a lefty, I always had fun with it through the years and it seemed to impress others when they learned I could throw from both sides.

I gave it no thought at the time, but in retrospect I've realized that I had a strong mind to overcome things— whatever they were—and when I put my mind to something, I achieved the results I'd hoped for. I never felt depressed by any of it. I never felt defeated or gave up on trying something new, I just adapted. I surely had enough setbacks already in my young life to have sulked around or given up, but I never did.

When spring came around I'd completely healed and tried out for the middle school Junior Varsity team, making the team in the dual role of pitcher— a right-handed pitcher— and shortstop. Even though we had to make the jump to the bigger field from the shorter Little League distances, my arm responded extremely well and there were no problems whatsoever.

But that 1976 baseball season for the Yankees was everything I'd imagined a baseball season to be, well... almost everything.

I'd become pretty astute at Yankees history by then, and got my hands on as many magazines or books having to do with them. And it didn't matter if they were new Yankees, old Yankees or even Yankees who'd been traded. I wanted to know everything about them. So when George Steinbrenner named Thurman team captain in April, I had a real good understand of its significance in Yankees history.

I'd held Babe Ruth and Lou Gehrig at the highest level of respect and admiration since Rizzuto started talking about them when I was bedridden. I've said it before, but Ruth and Gehrig were almost mythical players to me, bigger than life, really. There was something deeply magical about them, and when either name came up, I pictured them hitting home runs at Yankee Stadium and then later watching "The Babe Ruth Story," and listening intently to the emotional farewell speech given by Gehrig at Yankee Stadium.

When I first watched the grainy video from Gehrig's, "Luckiest man on the face of the earth," speech, I was mesmerized. Lou Gehrig knew he was dying and stood there in front of thousands of fans and teammates, facing his future and remembering his past with a poise and humility I'd never witnessed before. I think what Lou Gehrig had to say really touched me personally because of what I'd gone through as a child. I understood that having Perthes and then Osgood disease paled in comparison to being told you were going to die, but in a sense I could identify with it in ways, perhaps, that others couldn't. That may sound like a stretch, but it wasn't for me. And, like everything I'd watched, read, studied or researched, there was a lesson in it for me, with all of this coming to mind the day Thurman Munson was named Yankee captain.

I don't know if that title of being named Yankee captain had anything to do with their season, but after just three games played, the Yankees moved into first place and stayed there the entire season. I knew there was something special in that alone because I'd followed the standings in both leagues for years and knew that teams usually jockeyed for position throughout the long schedule. There was something to be said about a team nearly going wire-to-wire in first place. Good pitching, good defense, good depth, lack of injuries, all of that was needed for something like that to have happened.

All that happened with yet another new cast of characters. Gone were two starting pitchers, Pat Dobson and Doc Medich, acquired for Oscar Gamble, Ken Brett, Willie Randolph and Dock Ellis. Then when the Yankees traded Bobby Bonds to the Angels for speedster Mickey Rivers and pitcher Ed Figueroa, I had a lot to learn about our new team. I knew about Rivers, Gamble, Ellis and Brett, very little about Figueroa and nothing at all about 20 year old second baseman Willie Randolph. We already had Sandy Alomar as our second baseman, so Randolph was a name I barely paid attention to. Yankee fans know the rest of that story.

The blending of so many new players seemed to work. Rivers and Randolph combined for 80 stolen bases, Figueroa won 19 games and Ellis won 17, Gamble clubbed 17 homers in a part-time role, Roy White led the league with 104 runs scored and our power-hitting third baseman, Graig Nettles, led the league with 32 home runs. Despite all those contributions from up and down the lineup, it was Thurman Munson who was in his own league that year.

I attended my first Yankee game at Yankee Stadium that year with my parents, a tough, entertaining 6-5 loss to Oakland. And as I surveyed Yankee Stadium for the first time I was awed by its size and what I knew about its history. I couldn't help but think about all that, how Babe Ruth and Lou Gehrig and Mickey Mantle were right there on that field, and how magical that must have felt to be out there—even once. And as I waited for the starting lineups to be posted on the scoreboard, I prayed that Thurman was in the lineup as catcher. And he was.

I can't tell you enough about the day Thurman had, but when the game was over and he'd reached base in all five plate appearances I was convinced he'd done it for me. I took it personally that Thurman's three hits, two walks, and an RBI somehow came when I was in the stands, that the connection I'd felt with him was communicated in some spiritual way. And as crazy as that may sound to some, it was that game... that performance... that has stayed with me and has helped me stay focused on the biggest prize of all— Cooperstown.

I was finally getting to experience having my team in the playoffs, and watching that riveting playoff series against Kansas City, then to have the season end like it did was utterly disappointing. But that four game sweep by the Reds in the World Series— a series in which Thurman batted .529, showed the world what he was made of, what myself and others had know all along. Then for some reason the disrespect of Thurman began to show, starting with Reds manager Sparky Anderson.

It seemed to be the perfect time for an opposing World Series manager to show appreciation and even admiration for what Thurman had done in the series, but when Anderson said, "Munson is an outstanding player and he would hit .300 in the National League, but don't ever embarrass anybody by comparing him to Johnny Bench," that didn't sit well with me. Sure, the Yankees had been swept and Bench had a terrific series as well, but those ill-timed words affected Thurman Munson.

Theres's no words to describe how I felt when Thurman Munson was named the 1976 Most Valuable Player in the league after the World Series ended. I'm sure I was grinning from ear-to-ear and was happy for Thurman to be recognized in such a way. But I knew it wasn't going to be the one and only MVP award for Thurman, and I knew he'd produce over 2,000 hits before it was all over and lead the Yankees to several World Series titles. I thought for sure that Thurman Munson would one day be known as the greatest catcher the game had ever known, on the fast track to being immortalized in Cooperstown and couldn't wait for the next season to begin.

During that winter I was still seething over the comments Sparky Anderson made about Thurman, then when we signed Reggie Jackson in the off-season, the drama was just beginning.

But before all that, I felt even stronger for our chances than I had the year before. Before signing Reggie, Don Gullett, a tough lefty who beat the Yankees in game one of the World Series, was signed. Gullett was one of those under-the-radar types who always seemed to win, not a power pitcher, but one with great control and a variety of pitches, the perfect compliment to "Catfish" Hunter.

Of course I imagined Reggie standing inside the batters box at Yankee Stadium, ready to park one into the short right field porch, likely breaking the 61 homers hit by Roger Maris in 1961. Alongside Nettles, Chambliss and, of course, Thurman Munson, the Yankee lineup was going to be fun to watch.

Then when Reggie said, "This team, it all flows from me. I'm the straw that stirs the drink. Maybe I should say me and Munson, but he can only stir it bad," in a June 1977 article in Sport magazine, the drama started and never seemed to leave.

I tried to forget about it, but I couldn't. Sparky Anderson bothered me, but he wasn't a teammate of Thurman's, and Reggie really bothered me because he was. It bothered me also that two, high-profile baseball people had taken similar stands against Thurman— the low road when they could easily have taken the high road. I'd played on enough teams to know you had your teammates' back at all times, that getting along or at the very least respecting someone created the right chemistry for a team. And as much as I wanted to move on from the daily drama that soon followed the Yankees, I found myself opening to the back page of the *Newsday* sports page while delivering papers on Long Island, and couldn't believe the near-daily headlines relaying all the turmoil and disruptions throughout the organization.

I got no enjoyment from all that. What I wanted—and always wanted— was having a competitive team with all its stories centered on the game, the players and the pennant race, totally void of any drama.

It was right around the same time when lumps started forming under my knee caps that took my mind away from the Yankees problems to concentrate on mine. At first they were juts annoying to look at, then became painful to the touch or if someone bumped into me by accident. And like I'd done when I tried to hide my hip problem from my parents, I knew it was time to tell them what was going on.

When you've already had parts of your youth stolen out from under you, those immediate thoughts take you back in time. I'd fought my way like a trooper during that three year period, then underwent surgery on my broken arm and damaged eye—enough for any one person my age to have endured. But as the lumps became more pronounced and tender, I prayed that this one would go away on its own or with some sort of medication, that I'd be healed in time for the start of the baseball season.

When the diagnosis was revealed, I suppose it wasn't as dire as it could have been. I'd already learned all I needed to learn about *Legg-Calve-Perthes* disease, and now it was some other weird sounding disease I needed to learn about called *Osgood-Schlatter*. Turns out that *Osgood* wasn't good at all, but on a scale of one to ten, wasn't bad when compared to Perthes.

But, Osgood came with some strange dynamics that sort of put my mind into a quandary. We were told by the Doctor that rapid growing bones was the route of the cause and usually Osgood went away when the bones stopped growing. I knew as much as was to be expected for my age about the growth of the human body, and really had no idea when bones actually stopped growing. I only knew I was 14 years old and pretty much right at the normal growth spurt one would expect from anyone my age, and with what I'd been told, I thought it was possible I'd be sidelined until the day my bones stopped growing and that could be years away. As much as that bothered me, I kept it to myself.

Of course I wanted to keep growing. I wanted to fill out and get stronger like all the older boys had, to be able to compete and stay up on my competition, and that was the quandary I faced—to grow more meant the sidelines— to stop growing meant, well, I wasn't sure what it meant, but it couldn't be good. The good news was I wouldn't be needing a full-body cast or a wheelchair or crutches, only rest with no running or horseplay that I'd be missing the spring baseball season.

It was ironic that my good friend and teammate Matt Manzella would miss that year for the very same reason. That's right, both of us had been diagnosed with Osgood *at the very same time.* I wondered if this so called *disease*, was transmittable like the flu, and if it was, did Matt catch it from me or did I catch it from him? There was no talk from the grownups that such a thing was possible, and we weren't told to stay away from or not touch anyone, but what were the odds of something like that happening? I don't think either of us knew anyone else who'd ever had the disease and now there we were, together, not allowed to participate. It was a small consolation if any at all, being sidelined with a good friend, but we'd get through it together.

As usual, I thought such things through. Thurman Munson—along with my parents— had been a huge factor in helping me get through those early years. He'd been in the back of my mind so many times before when things got rough for me and with so many bad things continuing to happening to me, I still never felt sorry for myself. Watching Thurman play the game the way he did inspired me. I knew he got hurt all the time, I could see that for myself.

But he just sloughed it off all the time as if nothing had happened, no rolling around writhing in pain, no seeking out the camera and especially no drama. We had so much in common. I never wanted any attention from all that I'd endured, and drama wasn't even in my vocabulary. And now, thanks to Sparky Anderson and Reggie Jackson, I was in Thurman Munson's corner more than ever.

After that nasty fall in 7th grade and Osgood-Schlatter taking away my 8th grade season, I was ready for good things to happen in the 9th grade. Over the summer I grew another five inches in height, and despite what they'd said about Osgood-Schlatter occurring mostly during growth spurts, I wasn't concerned at all and was raring to go.

Along with the extra height came some extra strength, and I was throwing harder than I ever had before. Despite all that, coach Entler relegated me to being his fifth pitcher on the staff. I wasn't happy with that decision and felt I should have been higher in his rotation, but I worked hard and got my starts, winning my first six decisions and taking that perfect, 6-0 record into the seasons final game— the very same record Ron Guidry had for the Yankees just then

I'd felt like Ron Guidry must have felt when he took the mound for the Yankees that 1978 season, and thought about him whenever I took the ball, wanting badly for us to have identical records and to stay unbeaten. And as I stared into the catcher's glove of Craig Stapleton, he was Thurman Munson, and I was Ron Guidry.

While I had looked forward to ending the season with a win and end up with perfect won-loss record, Craig was looking for at least one more hit in that final game, a hit that would end his season with similar perfection to mine— a hit in every game. We'd talked about that right up to that game, wondering how it would feel if both of us achieved our goals. Turns out neither of us did. I lost that game and Craig went hitless.

It was another reminder that baseball didn't quite work out the way we wanted it to. It was an unforgiving game at times, a game that seemed to know exactly when to knock you off your perch, to reset things to a perfectly imperfect order, *to make you humble.*

But there was something extra-special in being recognized for a job well done, and when Craig and I were named co MVP's, I couldn't help but think of Thurman Munson winning his MVP award and how our lives continued to trend in the same direction.

Leaving Grand a year later for high school was tough on me. Having two high schools—John F. Kennedy High School and Mepham High School— meant splitting many of us up, and I knew that would be hard on all of us. We'd talked about it before, and we all knew that day was coming. And as I became a Sophomore at JFK, my good friends and the core of our infield was headed to Mepham.

Losing Mike Albanese (3B), John Collins (SS) and Matt Manzella (2B) was unthinkable to me. That infield gobbled up so many ground balls that helped me countless times, I knew I'd miss them— both on and off the field. And at Grand I was one of the big men on campus and starting over at JFK would change all that. I was starting over with new coaches to impress and new people to compete against— most being upperclassman who'd be stronger and bigger than I was. And JFK was an "A" Division School that made things even that much harder, and I knew it wouldn't be easy to make that team.

But I did have some things going for me. My friend and neighbor Tommy Pfingst – a star centerfielder and senior on the squad—was in my corner big time, pulling for me and putting in a good word with coach Senior, as well as star pitcher/left field senior Gene Collins – who had played Little League ball with me on the Indians – and made me feel right at home, always encouraging me. I truly believe that because of their support and with some good tryouts and scrimmages, I was able to make that great team.

That team was loaded with Tommy, Gene, Steve Rogers, Joel Weiss, Mike Radvansky and my good friend, Woody Most. They all could hit the long ball and they were incredible to watch each day. I pitched out of the bullpen and played shortstop when Steve pitched and I played third base in other games. We won eight of our last nine to squeak into the sectionals, then totally dominated the first two games until running into Levittown's lefty Tom Epple and his 90 mile per hour fastball. It was no wonder he'd later be drafted by the St. Louis Cardinals, spending parts of seven seasons in the minors but never even getting a cup of coffee with the big club.

Of course I turned much of my attention to the Yankees after that, watching as many games as I could, checking out the standings and the stats. Never had I been happier following two straight World Series championships, especially that 1978 season when they trailed the Red Sox by 14 games in the middle of July. I thought back to what Rizzuto said about the 49' Yankees and never lost hope. I'd followed enough baseball to know it was never over in July, no matter how bleak it may have seemed. And as they crawled back into it by sweeping a four game series at Fenway in, "The Boston Massacre," they'd erased that entire deficit, then grabbed the lead.

I attended that last regular season game of the season with Tommy Cespites at Yankee Stadium against Cleveland, hoping the Yankees one game lead would hold up and I'd be there for the celebration. And while I was a bit bummed out when they lost, 9-2 and the Red Sox shutout Toronto, I think my love for baseball went up a level after that.

I'm not going to recap that historic game against Boston, or even dive into the playoffs and World Series. I won't even go into the season Thurman Munson had or any of the Yankees drama. All I knew was a dynasty had been born, and I was there to witness it with Thurman Munson on top of the baseball world.

Chapter 8
The Show Must Go On

"We turned the news on and started listening to the details. I couldn't believe it. I stood there, stunned at what I was hearing, trying to process what they were saying about Thurman."

I was only 16 when Thurman Munson died. It was between my sophomore and junior years in high school, years when I really started to understand what Thurman Munson meant to the Yankees.

My friend, Jerry Reynolds called me that day and asked if I'd heard the news about Thurman Munson. I had no idea what he was talking about, so when he said, "Thurman just died in a plane crash," I thought he was joking.

Being young and foolish at times, we'd always joked around with each other, but this wasn't funny at all. If this was a joke, he'd gone too far. There was no humor in what he just told me, but I hoped it was a joke, and that after breathing a sigh of relief when he admitted it was, I'd reprimand him then find a way to make him pay for it later.

Then as Jerry started telling me he'd heard the announcement while watching a Mets game, I started thinking maybe he wasn't kidding around. I could tell by the shaky sound of his voice that something awful had happened, and as I listened further to his words I felt more confused because what he was saying wasn't adding up to me.

Thurman Munson was invincible in my book— almost like Superman — the rock of the team and the most reliable player in baseball. He never missed a game, or took a day off or even got hurt. I thought Jerry made a mistake and hoped that he had gotten it wrong. But as he went on with the few details he'd heard, I knew he was right...

We turned the news on and started listening to the details—almost word-for-word to what Jerry had said. I couldn't believe it. I just stood there, stunned at what I was hearing, trying to understand fully what had happened. And as the news report sounded more like a bad dream than reality, a thousand thoughts came to mind.

The suddenness of it all was hard for me to process and my thoughts were a jumbled mess with a randomness I couldn't keep up with or seem to be able to control. My first thought was wondering how the Yankees would get through this. Then my mind was replaying back memories— my personal memories— of Thurman as a rookie, listening to Rizzuto talk about him with such flair. His performances in the World Series, the connection I had to him when I was crippled, his baseball cards and his clutch hits.

I thought back to when I was little, when everything was great, when you really didn't know about the problems going on around you and in the world and how knowing Thurman Munson gave me something very special and *very personal* to look forward to. And as the years went by, how that innocence of youth started to fade away and problems started to arise that affected you deeply, that for each passing year those problems intensified and that bubble of safety began to erode.

My dream was to play professional baseball, but I always knew what a long shot that was. I was 16 and in love with the game, a fanatic about baseball, a fanatic about Thurman. They'd reached the pinnacle of baseball with no end in sight, and I finally understood what Rizzuto was talking about from those glory years of Yankee teams past.

I delivered papers on Long Island— *Newsday*— and read every inch of everything I could get my hands on about baseball and the Yankees. I watched every game, I listened to the games on the radio, I studied and learned and rooted for the guys I admired most. Thurman was *team captain,* a title of reverence and acclaim. He wasn't supposed to die...

When Thurman started talking about wanting to be traded to Cleveland to be closer to home and wanted out of New York, that was the last thing I wanted to hear from him and it made me very upset. Just thinking about him playing for another team in another city bugged me to no end, and I wondered why he didn't seem more grateful for all that he had being a Yankee.

I thought he was being selfish, and the fact that he seemed fine with leaving such an excellent team, one that would compete for the pennant for years to come, gnawed on me. And go to Cleveland? They'd lost 90 games two straight years and never were in the pennant race. None of that made any sense to me. I was a kid, what did I know?

I couldn't understand his reasoning at the time, and did think about his family and wanting to be closer to home. But I didn't have any personal relationship with any of his three children or his wife or friends and likely never would. I was 16 years old and thought more of how his death would devastate the team as far as losing its competitive edge. Thurman Munson couldn't be replaced, that I knew and was concerned about. Oh sure, they'd run out another catcher and put him somewhere in the lineup, but replacing all the intangibles that made Thurman who he was, never missing a game, clutch hitting, the attitude, the confidence and swagger, all of it was never going to happen. And I've got to be honest— I don't remember shedding a lot of tears when I heard the news. Maybe I was just too stunned to react that way. I don't know.

But now I know and have shed some tears for Thurman—lots of them. I'm a husband, a father and a grandfather. My family is everything to me, a baseball family. I coached my sons from Little League on up. I watched them mature and become men and have their own families. Now I know exactly why Thurman wanted to be traded to Cleveland, and that's exactly why he means more to me now than ever. I suppose I should have been more sensitive to all that back then, but I didn't know much about his upbringing and having such a tumultuous relationship with his dad. There'd been nothing but love from my parents, love and encouragement and direction and hope. Sure, we had our problems like most families around us had, but at the end of the day, we were a unit, a loving, caring family unit that always had your back.

If I'd known all that at the time, I would have viewed Thurman Munson with a deeper understanding of all that and not been so selfish. I would have looked at him as more than just a baseball player, *because he was much more than that to me.* He had a family too, one he wanted to be with.

I cut out Bill Gallo's drawing of Thurman from the New York Daily News, Thurman's head bowed from the heavens, eyes closed, a reverent, almost apologetic look on this face as he listens to two boys with their heads down, one saying to the other, "Naw, Yuchie— I just don't feel like playin' ball today— a drawing I've kept all these years later.

There was an outpouring of emotion that day from coast-to-coast and into the day Thurman was buried. But when the Yankees decided to return from Canton following Thurman's burial earlier in the day to play a nationally televised game against Baltimore at Yankee Stadium, that seemed surreal to just about everybody. But everyone knew it was what Thurman would have wanted— *The Show Must Go On-* and so they played the game, one of the most memorable games in my lifetime.

I must go back in time for a moment here, a moment to the day Bobby Murcer had been traded to San Francisco for Bobby Bonds— a moment that would have a profound affect on this tribute game against Baltimore.

From the moment that trade was made, I knew Bobby Murcer would be back one day, back being a Yankee. I followed him from San Francisco to Chicago, always rooting for him and hoping he was happy, but knowing deep-down he belonged a Yankee. I thought of him the three straight years the Yankees were in the World Series, then thought of him even more when they won the last two.

For a player, there's nothing better than being on a World Series championship team and getting a World Series ring, and I felt bad that Bobby hadn't gotten his. But after that game against Baltimore— *Bobby Murcer's game*—I doubt he'd ever trade that one memorable game in for any World Series ring.

I could go along with the idea of a Divine Intervention being in place that night, but had never paid attention to what that might mean. And while emotions ran deep, and we rooted for something great to happen— something way out of the ordinary— Bobby Murcer provided just that.

Some said Bobby Murcer was in the right place at the right time that night, that the five runs he drove in— including the final two to win the game with two outs in the bottom of the ninth— was nothing more than good luck. There was talk of how *improbable* such a game could be, how one player— one player alone— could drive in all five runs his team would score and to do so on such an emotionally charged field. And as the world tried to process a possible *Divine Intervention,* the word, *impossible* hadn't figured into any of it.

Sometimes emotions helps you refocus in a different kind of way, and maybe that day Bobby Murcer's emotions made all the difference in the outcome of that memorable game. I don't know. What I do know is watching that television camera panning the crowd when the winning run scored, and seeing everyone crying at that magical moment. That's when I got choked up.

It was such an odd feeling then because the cheering just wouldn't stop. And as I watched and listened to the cheers grow stronger and stronger, I didn't want it to end, didn't want that surging noise to ever end. I kept hoping it wouldn't stop, and the longer it went, the longer I believed it would go on forever. When the cheering finally subsided and eventually did end, I realized at that very moment that Thurman was really gone.

Chapter 9
The Tryout

"I seemed to have lost my purpose right around that time, and Thurman's death had no bearing on the funk that started taking me down."

My junior season was a rough one. We lost too many good players to graduation and struggled to compete with the rest of that strong league. We added my good friend Dan Kouw – a terrific pitcher who had transferred from Holy Trinity— and Craig moved up from the JV squad, hitting like he always had.

I'd been voted as team co-captain along with Senior pitcher and stud right fielder Joel Weiss, another player on that Reds team that beat me in 1975. That was quite an honor, knowing that teammates saw me as a leader.

I wasn't the most vocal guy on the team, and was much more comfortable with leading by example. I followed a simple formula that included working hard, rooting for others, taking direction from our coaches and never giving up. I strived for excellence and took my title seriously, grateful for that opportunity. And I took my role as leadoff batter to get us off to a good start every game, to get on base and get the rally started. At seasons end I did well enough to be named Most Valuable Player again – an honor I was truly grateful for.

We hoped for much better things my senior season but played .500 ball if we were lucky. I batted leadoff again, but Craig was unstoppable at the plate and earned team MVP.

I was again named team co-captain with my friend, left handed pitcher Terry White. Terry's older brother Tommy pitched at St. Johns with John

Franco and Frank Viola and made it all the way to the college World Series in Omaha, Nebraska.

Another year not making the playoffs for us was frustrating. Being a senior you wanted your last year to be a memorable one, a season filled with competitive games well past the regular season. And while that never materialized, our season ended on a good note, a 5-2 win over Berner High School of Massapequa.

I took the mound that day wanting my season and high school baseball career to end on a good note. And as the innings went by and we built our lead, I looked around that field every inning knowing that each pitch I threw was one less pitch of my high school career. As I came off the mound in-between innings I thought back to my teammates who'd been there before and those with me now, then took a few seconds longer to look at each player who'd made a play for me for me in the field. It was a subtle gesture, really. Nobody knew what was going on inside of me, but I was deeply grateful for all of it. If it had been possible for me to bear down even more than I always had, I think I did that day. Yes, I wanted more than anything to end my high school baseball career with a victory, but more than that, I wanted all my fellow seniors to go out as winners.

I'd learned how to throw the knuckleball years earlier from Al Pabisch, but had never been brave enough to throw one in a game. I was a control pitcher and proud of that. I'd worked hard for years on hitting the catcher's spot, and throwing a knuckleball, well, nobody knew where it might go. But with Craig's mom (another prominent figure later on) and dad – Mickey and Pat Stapleton behind the backstop encouraging me the whole way—I looked in at Craig to get the sign for the next pitch.

There were two out in that last inning with their best hitter at the plate when Craig gave the sign to throw the knuckler. I think I smiled at first then shook off Craig's sign. But when he gave it again with more emphasis, I knew he wasn't kidding around. I stepped off the mound to think it over, then toed the rubber. I took a good look at that ball nestled in the webbing of my glove, rotated it around a few times, then positioned my fingers around it before nodding confidently to Craig.

When that pitch left my hand and the ball fluttered and danced ever so slowly as I tried following its path, it moved and shifted like a knuckleball should. I couldn't tell if it was going outside, rising or dropping, but when that ball finally passed home plate and entered Craig's glove safely, the "Strike three," shouted by the umpire was music to my ears, and we went out winners.

But some of the music had died inside of me with Thurman's passing. My final two years of high school ball were sandwiched right around Thurman's death. I'd still followed the Yankees and always would, but there was a void that I think everyone felt. I still watched with passion but clearly our leader was gone. I was happy that Rick Cerone had a fabulous year in 1980, but nobody could do what Thurman could do. It was horrible watching Kansas City finally stomp us in 80, and the Dodgers finally beating us the following year. I'm convinced none of that would have happened if Thurman was still there, and convinced he never would have left New York for Cleveland.

Of course I had college on my mind and had for some time heading into my final summer playing in the Senior Babe Ruth League. I was thrilled to be playing for Craig's dad— a police officer and a man I admire greatly— for the third straight season, and that baseball wasn't quite yet over for me or for others on that team. And how could it be? My dream was still to become a major league ball player, and despite any of the odds against such a thing happening, that dream remained in the back of my mind, and that some random scout would one day— just by chance— stop by and watch us play, then be impressed enough to sign me to a contract. That didn't sound so far-fetched to me because I believed in such things. Part of the dream is *to dream,* and I held that dream close to the vest... I wanted to be a Yankee.

I was just 18 and started to believe that there was something to that way of thinking, that karma was real and so was prayer. I'd been a living miracle in some ways, a survivor against the odds. And while I never dwelled on any such thoughts for long, things were taking shape in my mind. Then when coach Stapleton called me, Craig, Mike Albanese and Terry White together for a meeting, we could tell it was for something more than any team meetings we'd had before. He'd arranged a tryout for the four us at Yankee Stadium, you can imagine how I felt.

Coach Stapleton told us he'd worked with a Yankee scout on a tryout for the four of us at Yankee Stadium, that there'd be others there with us, all trying out for the New York Yankees. Holy cow!

Of course that was all I thought about over the next few days. I was overjoyed and couldn't wait to happen, nervous and excited at once. But as that day approached, and it became harder to contain the excitement, I noticed we had a game scheduled the night before the tryout and it was my turn to pitch.

I'd given it my all every time I pitched, and because I'd usually go the distance, my arm needed a few days to return to normal after a game. Ever since I'd been told about the Yankees tryout, I envisioned myself on the Yankee Stadium mound, fresh and ready to go.

But I was always a team first guy—always— and I understood the Yankees tryout really was a once-in-a-lifetime opportunity, a day to showcase my talent in front of those in the know. And as I wrestled with the quandary I was in and warmed up on the sidelines for the game, Coach approached me. I remember him telling me that he understood if I didn't want to pitch that night, and that I could save my arm for the tryout the next day. But I didn't take much time to answer him. I thought for a second and told him it was my turn and I was going to be there for the team. He asked again, and I told him I was sure.

The complete game shutout I tossed that night was barely on my mind the next day as we headed to Yankee Stadium for the tryout. We were all pretty tired but fired up and ready to go during the 40 minute drive from Long Island. When we got there they reviewed our positions with us and I was told that I could either pitch in the bullpen or tryout at another position where I would also get to hit. My arm was pretty sore from the night before, but I couldn't pass up the opportunity to actually get to hit at Yankee stadium. I chose the infield.

Major League baseball was on strike at the time, but there I was, getting loose on the field and running laps around the warning track inside that massive stadium where so many greats had played. Even knowing I had to stay focused on the task at hand, I couldn't help myself. Babe Ruth was here. Lou Gehrig... Joe DiMaggio... Thurman Munson.

I headed out to shortstop to field grounders along with just one other player, then noticed a few others stationed at third while the majority of players gathered near second base. I found out later that they chose second base so the shorter throw would be easier to make, to even hide any arm-strength deficiencies one might have. But I found that to border on ridiculous. These were major league scouts we were performing in front of, certainly they'd recognized flaws or strengths hundreds of times before, and nothing could be hidden from them. I introduced myself to the other shortstop, and he said, "Hi Im Walt... Walt Weiss.

Turns out it was the very same Walt Weiss who would later win the 1989 "Earthquake" World Series along with his Oakland A's teammates Rickey Henderson, Mark McGwire and Jose Canseco. As if that wasn't the only name to remember, a young black player at third named Shawon Dunston was firing missiles to first base, holding every ground ball he fielded until a scout yelled, "Now let it go Shawon!" I held my own on the field, but I was no Walt Weiss or Shawon Dunston— and they were the two who stood out.

Despite a poor round of hitting his first time through, Dunston started hitting balls into the left field stands— lots of them. It was no surprise to me when he went on to a stellar career with the Cubs. And then Weiss lined pitch after pitch into the gaps and across the field. After a while he turned around to hit left-handed, surprising me by hitting hard line drives seemingly at will. *What a sweet swing*, I thought.

When it was my turn to hit I got off to a terrible start. Perhaps I was trying too hard, but soon I settled down and started smoking line drives into the gap like my hero Thurman had. It was satisfying to say the least, and I was very thankful that I turned it around a bit. They had us run the 60 yard dash, and I was in the lead when the guy next to me separated himself from the pack for the last 20 yards. I held my own and didn't feel too bad about it.

When the tryout ended they read the names off for those they'd be inviting back the next day for a scrimmage. And as happy players heard their names being called, the list grew shorter and shorter until finally the last name was called. I gave it everything I had in that tryout, and am forever grateful to Pat Stapleton for making that happen.

But I'd thought ahead of all that. I wanted to keep playing baseball after high school and had been accepted to New Haven, Connecticut for college, then written to their Division II baseball coach. He sent me a positive response and said that he was looking forward to meeting me and having me tryout for the team.

I should have been excited about moving to a new area and taking the next step of my baseball journey, but mentally I wasn't ready. Going from Grand Avenue Junior High to John F. Kennedy senior high was a big enough jump but at least I knew many people there. There was a comfort I'd come to know and didn't want to let go of yet. I liked having my friends around, having family around, just knowing they were there. That's when I decided to switch gears and enrolled at our local Nassau Community College.

I knew I had an excellent chance at making the baseball team and thought I was prepared to make my mark there. Things didn't turn out so well. I completed that first semester with a 2.7 GPA, then at the start of the second semester I withdrew to go to work for a mason with my good friend Jim Donachie.

I seemed to have lost my purpose right around that time, and Thurman's death had no bearing on the funk that started taking me down. For the first time since my recovery, I didn't have a baseball team to look forward to playing on, had passed up on college and felt trapped. Baseball and my faith always kept me grounded but now I had neither. I started hanging in the bars night after night, drinking 'til closing with no sense of direction. Sure, I seemed like a happy patron, drinking with "friends" where "everybody knows your name." But even those people gathered at the bar with me seemed to be able to drink and party and still move forward with a goal in mind. I was not only stuck... I was going in reverse.

I still attended church occasionally with my friend Rob Esposito, but even that didn't pull me out. Even knowing that Rob had broken his neck immediately upon graduation two years earlier and the doctors said he would never walk again did little to acknowledge that spirituality and belief system I'd come to know. But we were in church together just two years later, Rob proving them wrong. As hard as it seemed to be, I still managed to pray and kept believing that God had a plan for my life.

I wanted to change, but that spiral I was in kept spinning me towards the abyss. My brother, Tim was the one person who really took notice to my new lifestyle, and he didn't like it. I should have listened to him and I knew I needed to get a grip on things.

One day I'd had enough. I looked in the mirror and was horrified at what I'd become. How could I have lost the mindset and beliefs that had become such a key part of me in such a short amount of time? How could I abandon all I'd known, to fight the fight and keep on fighting? How could I go home every night, purposeless, somewhat defeated, even mildly depressed and do it again tomorrow?

It was right then that I decided to try and stop the drinking and carousing and prayed for a good woman to come into my life. I wanted my normal life back.

Chapter 10
Southeastern Academy

"I needed to get far away from everything that was going on and I needed to straighten myself out, because nothing was working out."

By the end of 1982 things hadn't changed that much for me. I was still going out early and coming home late from the bar. It didn't seem to matter how many times I promised to change my behavior and way of life. I'd just circle back to the drinking and carousing and would promise myself the next day that today was the day. But I didn't.

It's funny how the mind works. There I was giving myself a message to stop and then falling victim to what I'd created. It didn't seem to matter how many times I looked at myself in the mirror with disgust and anger, and wondering what had happened to me. It seemed the more I wanted to clean things up, the further away I got. I had gone from 180 pounds of solid muscle to 120 pounds of despair. It was bleak, and I was in serious trouble.

I'd noticed that every time in my life when things were going well or going sour, some life-changing event rocked my world— events that altered my life's course and would inevitably change my life for the better. But that was hard to see or even understand or follow that back then. I just wanted my life back again, and despite myself, I continued the hard prayer for that to happen. And soon enough, another major event—an automobile accident— almost killed me, and, in a strange sort of way, was what helped get me back on course.

But just a few months before that accident I was a drivers helper working for a company with my friend Nicky Paris, that supplied pizza ingredients across much of the Northeast. I was looking forward to ending my shift and attending an Adam Ant concert at the Roseland Ballroom with Craig later that night.

We'd worked all day making deliveries in the driving rain, then headed home on a country road clearly marked with a "Stop" sign for vehicles coming the other way. When we entered the intersection a driver coming the other way failed to stop and hadn't slowed down when she clipped the rear of our truck, hurtling us into a gully, flipping our truck over and landing on the side that I was sitting on.

It was a miracle neither of us were injured, but the driver of the other car had blood pouring from her face. She was in rough shape. Later on our company put us up in hotel that night and paid for our dinner. I missed two days of work but was lucky there were no injuries aside from a sore back that healed on its own.

It was two months later when I was just turning my car into the driveway of my friend, Chris Guthrie's house when another car decided to pass on the left and directly into the driver's side where I was sitting, and where the impact occurred.

The impact bent the steering wheel and the door completely wrapped around my body like it had been fitted to me. I somehow managed to open the door and poured myself out onto the lawn, lying there in pain and waiting for an ambulance to arrive. This time there were injuries.

I suffered a few cuts to my face but nothing was broken. But injuries to my back required me to be put into traction for five days with neck and back trauma. Later on after I healed, we sued the rental car company (and settled out of court) that had rented their vehicle to an illegal alien with no drivers license.

That second accident started putting things into perspective for me. I started asking myself why my life had been spared yet another time. They said I should have died when I fell from the roof of the school and now they'd said it again. And I could have died after the first car accident in November as well. None of it added up to me. I had been through so much turmoil in my life. I felt betrayed by certain 'friends.' I was lonely, confused, and angry and I was desperate for a change. I drove the six miles to Jones

Beach all alone on a freezing cold day. So many crazy thoughts were running through my mind. And then it hit me... that great big Atlantic Ocean staring back at me made me and my problems seem so small. I threw a rock in the ocean, gave thanks to the Lord and vowed that from that day on my drinking days that were wasting my life away were over... really over."

Within months a postcard from the Southeastern Academy in Florida arrived in the mail addressed to me, seeking applicants for Travel & Tourism. With all that happened in my life, I knew I needed a change of scenery, so I filled it out and sent it in. I knew this was meant especially for me.

About a week later my mom woke me up to tell me a woman was on the phone from some academy in Florida and wanted to talk to me. I sprung out of bed, ran to the phone and introduced myself to her. She said she was so and so from Southeastern Academy and had my returned postcard in front of her. After a while she set up an appointment for me to meet with her. She came to our house told me all about the school and lined up several brochures across the table. I was really excited about the opportunity. I had the money I'd received from the lawsuit and could afford the move. I signed on the dotted line.

I couldn't believe how quickly their response was. Only God does that. Only God does that... It was just a postcard that came in the mail, and maybe it went out across the entire neighborhood. I don't know, but it was an answered prayer for me. My mom or siblings could have just thrown out that letter when it arrived, and if they had done that, I would never have known. I needed to get far away from Long Island, I just had to. I needed to get far away from everything that was going on and I needed to straighten myself out, because nothing was working out. Just troubles in life. A lot of sorrow. A lot of hard things going on in my family that wasn't all peaches and cream, some of it is very personal, very, very personal. And by the grace of God, that letter showed up when I needed it most.

My parents asked me if I was sure this was what I wanted to do and I said absolutely, it sounded terrific to see the world, travel & tourism, become a flight attendant, become a desk clerk at a hotel, work for the airlines. Whatever job it was they all sounded right for me. I'd worked at a hotel with my brother as a bellhop on weekends when I was in high school, so I had an idea what the hospitality business was like. I enjoyed helping guests with luggage and of course the tips that came with the job.

I could have staggered the 12 week training course into six weeks at home and six on site, but I chose the option of all 12 weeks on site. I couldn't have spent another six days in Long Island let alone six weeks, so off to Florida it was for me.

I always knew that God had a plan for me. Even through the tough times. When I was a kid it wasn't all choir boy and altar boy stuff. I definitely had my rough times. And now with all the accidents and second and third and even fourth chances at life, I wanted to settle down, to really settle down and Florida seemed like the best place I'd be doing it. Here I was, 20 years old having never flown before, and when I got on that plane and it took flight, I never felt so free in my life.

At the same time a young lady named Suzette had recieved the very same postcard where she lived in upstate, New York, and had enrolled in the same 12 week proram I was in. I knew nothing of her, or her background or what her likes and dislikes were. All I knew was the moment I spotted her on campus I wanted to meet her. I had regained 40 pounds from eating well and taking care of myself, exercising and doing 200 pushups a day. All of my confidence and sense of self-worth had returned.

I don't recall doing anything clever or out of the ordinary to try and get her to notice me. We met finally about halfway through the course, just before her 20th birthday. She was helping a friend of mine with some class work and just started a casual conversation. She was just so beautiful with the most perfect broad smile and a very sweet disposition. I got the courage up to ask her out, and we dated a few times after that, many dates going out dancing and having a ball. We were inseparable.

Turns out she got hired by Northeastern Airways as a reservationist before the course even ended with a transfer to my neck of the woods on Long Island. The airline industry was anxiously looking for people coming out of our school, and getting hired before graduating seemed to be quite common. In mid December we both graduated, she flew home to Bath, and I flew home to Long Island. On Christmas night she flew to Long Island in a terrible snow storm to start her job, and I picked her up at MacArthur Airport in Ronkonkoma, driving through the same storm she had flown into. Eventually she secured an interview for me with the same company and just like that I was hired for the same reservationist job on Long Island. Suzette was friends with two others from school who'd also been hired by the same airline for jobs at the same location as us. It seemed to be a natural fit so the four of us rented an apartment near work in Patchogue.

It didn't take long for that number to drop to three. I think the parents of one of the girls wouldn't let her move in and it wasn't too long after that when the other girl moved out, leaving the place to me and Suzette. We knew, and we felt we were meant to be together and decided to get married soon after, both certain of our future together. God had a plan, and we were destined to be together as one and within months we were married. We were busy at work for a while, but then the bottom fell out. I went from crazy busy all day booking seats to sitting there for eight hours doing nothing. The company expanded too quickly, and that strategy wasn't working.

I wasn't happy because I needed to work. I hated being idle and enjoyed it when it was busy. I don't like sitting around doing nothing or talking to other employees for more than a few minutes. I wanted to earn my pay and be productive and it wasn't happening.

We both saw the writing on the wall for Northeastern. They got power-hungry from the initial surge of business and allowed it to influence their strategy. When they expanded too quickly and things went south, we decided we'd had enough and gave our two week notices. We got our final paychecks right up to the end, but when the company folded a few weeks later, there were plenty of others who didn't.

Despite all the ups and downs we'd experienced at Northeastern, I knew my prayers had been answered. Of course I'd noted the roundabout manner in which that prayer found its wings. From the accident to the lawsuit to the letter and moving to Florida was quite a journey for a prayer to make. This wasn't the first time I'd followed the path a prayer takes, but it was likely the first time I'd really understood how to read the signs life gives you.

But there was more on the way for us. We moved in with my brother Roy, his wife Laura and their beautiful daughters Dawn and Tara where I took a job as an assistant at a gas station right around the corner. I did that for a while and then I got my own station that was situated in a bad area out on Islip where my employee was robbed at gunpoint and later by somebody brandishing a knife. That's when we decided that was it, we were moving back to Florida.

We both worked at a construction company Suzette's dad owned in Florida. I'd learned to work with my hands doing masonry, but her dad started teaching me carpentry and building. I wasn't excited about the job and Suzette wasn't crazy about office work, so we packed it up again after three months and headed back to my parents house on Long Island.

Neither of us had a job lined up but my friend Chris Guthrie had started a flooring business and when his helper left, he asked me if I was interested in taking his place. Not only did I take that job, I opened my own flooring business a year later and ended up being in the business for 25 years.

I loved being out to the different homes and meeting new people all the time. Every job was different. One day it could be a living room or dining room, the next day it might be a stairway. I enjoyed working with different types of carpet, working with my hands and getting a good physical day from the labor required.

With all this going on, we were married early in 1984, then our first son, Tommy, came along by years end. When Danny was born four years later, we decided to move upstate to be closer to Suzette's parents and her siblings Missy, Sherman and Matthew.

My family loved Suzette from the moment they met her, and she loved them. Of course my hope was that her family would welcome me in as mine had welcomed Suzette, and I had that on my mind the day we'd met. I'd known ahead of time these were people of great faith, mindful Christians in every sense of the word, and I was eager to be around that.

Prayer changes everything. God's grace and mercy can lead you *to a peace that passes all understanding,* and that's what I felt when I first met them. Larry and Brenda would have a profound effect on my life.

Chapter 11
Fields of Dreams

"But the pain was all part of the deal one makes with the game of baseball, that sometimes reaching a dream and other times experiencing a nightmare is separated by the thinnest of margins."

Throughout the chaos and all the moving back and forth between Florida and Long Island, I kept an ever watchful eye on the Yankees and, for that matter, all that was going on in baseball.

The toughest part of any one season to follow was the ending to that 1979 season right after Thurman's accident. There was a part of me that half expected Thurman to take the field, both a desperate and wishful part of me that wanted to turn back the clock and set things back to the way they were, the way things were supposed to be. I'd smile a little smile to myself, then nod as I pictured Thurman behind the plate. And while such occasional daydreams had me lost in the past for those scant few seconds, it was the present situation with Thurman Munson for the Hall of Fame that had me concerned.

There was special clause to the Hall of Fame charter following a player's death, the normal five year waiting period following retirement being waived, making Thurman eligible at the next vote. Perhaps I was a bit naive at the time, but I had no doubts at all that baseball would do the right thing by voting Thurman in. By "the right thing" I expected the voters to recognize Thurman's on field contributions, all the hardware and trophies and rings he'd won—and earned— and not going soft with some "pity" vote because of his death.

But there was nothing soft about the voters. When the votes were cast and the announcement came down it was utterly surprising to me when only 15.5% of the writers penciled in Thurman. Hard as it was for me, I gave them a pass this one time. I knew it was rare for a player to get in on the first go around, and in following the path to the Hall by others who'd made it, those numbers usually went up every year until the 75% needed was achieved. I became rather curious to the unique voting process and even frustrated on how and why players with Hall of Fame credentials had to wait it out like this.

I started with Bob Gibson— the only player inducted that 1981 year— and studied an impressive list of other "sure bet" players on that ballot, some—like the late Gil Hodges and Phillies star outfielder Richie Ashburn— at the very end of the 15 year window the Hall "graciously" allows players to remain on a ballot.

It seemed unconceivable placing the Hodges family and Richie Ashburn into such torturous and anxious situations every year, especially the voting history given Hodges, an agonizingly close 60.1% of the vote his top year to date. With but two years to go before that window closed for good, I had a sense that Gil Hodges— and especially Richie Ashburn and his 35%— would unfairly become casualties of whatever politics they were playing instead of receiving an honor they so richly deserved. Furthermore, it was inexplicable trying to comprehend how and why others on the ballot for the first time like Harmon Killebrew, Juan Marichal and an all-star roster bursting with players who belonged, hadn't hit the magic 75% for induction.

I wanted to get a sense of where Killebrew and Marichal— slam dunk Hall of Famers— stood in relationship to Thurman, a reference point I hoped would help me feel better about the lack of respect the writers had given Thurman. But it wasn't even close. Both players had four times what Thurman received.

Certainly it was a wakeup call for me and I was deeply concerned about Thurman's future chances. With what I'd learned about the voting process I had a feeling the struggle was on and I wanted to do something about it, but who was I? I wasn't connected in any way, shape or form to baseball, didn't know a soul who could help or even listen to my concerns.

But as 1981 turned into 1982 and 1982 into 1983, the love for Thurman nearly dissolved at the voting table. That I was embarrassed by the 15.5% he received his first year on the ballot paled to the 6.3% and 4.8% he'd received the following two years. I knew enough now about the voting process to understand that the writing was on wall for any player trending down. This was not good.

Of course I felt bad that Gil Hodges and Richie Ashburn had been passed over for induction on their final years of eligibility but I wasn't surprised. There was such an unfairness to the whole thing, an unrighteous, almost pompous attitude I felt exuding from a panel of voters who seemed clueless and even heartless. They'd taken a pass on Gil Hodges and Richie Ashburn and others before them, and that made no sense to me.

I'd managed to work some free time in every now and then to the basic research I'd started years earlier while watching the all-star game, a fun exercise I enjoyed and looked forward to doing. That initial research— albeit it cursory — had really set the wheels in motion for a passion that sort of bordered on detective work. I'd always been fascinated by any set of numbers footing down or across that made sense to an outcome— especially with baseball.

But now that the Hall of Fame future for Thurman was looking bleak, charting stats for fun took a serious turn. I'd need to go all out now, to disseminate as much as I could find, to delve deep inside the numbers of other Hall of Fame players and to chart and graph and do whatever it would take to prove to the world what I already knew about Thurman.

It would be another 20 years before *Baseball Reference* changed the landscape for baseball researchers, and what was available at the time was, *The Baseball Encyclopedia*, a massive publication that seemed to have just about everything I was looking for.

• • •

This was also way before the introduction of new metrics used today like WAR (Wins Against Replacement) and OPS (On Base + Slugging). What we had was what we'd all known our whole lives, the major stats of Runs, Hits, RBI and Batting Average used to best evaluate a players offense. What it didn't have was what I wanted the most.

There were no statistics given to clutch hitting, situational hitting and even less regarding defense or durability and I had no way of uncovering this results. But I knew any parts of these categories and others would make for a stronger, more convincing case for Thurman. And while I longed for such numbers to be readily available, I took things as far as I could with what I had to work with, starting with the number of games those Hall of Fame catcher's had played in during their careers.

As I concocted a plan— at least in my mind— to chart all the available stats for Hall of Fame catchers, I was totally surprised upon discovering there'd been only seven Hall of Fame catcher's in the history of the game, with two of them—Roger Bresnahan and Buck Ewing— playing mostly before 1901— the first season The Baseball Encyclopedia referenced team and individual statistics, leaving just five players to research.

But that great plan to conduct the research I was eager to pursue went on hold and stayed there for not just a few weeks or a few months, but for years, decades even. I won't say that life got in the way because life was pretty great and extremely busy. My flooring business was thriving and by the time I got home from work, my attention and whatever energy I had left from the day went to helping Suzette with the boys.

I went to bed most nights exhausted, and some nights—many nights— I wanted to just jump out of bed and burn the midnight oil doing my research, but knew I'd be needing the rest required for the type of job I was in. In time— *God's time*— was the phrase I kept close to the vest.

But playing baseball was another story. Since a young boy I'd been around the game, and when summer ended couldn't wait for spring to arrive and to get out the glove and bat and get ready for another season. The game was really in my blood and always had been, and because of that I'd played semi-pro on Long Island for five years, winning the Nassau County

· · ·

Championship in July of 1988, just before moving upstate for good.

I had some memories from high school when I took the mound against the O'Shea Slammers for that championship game. That I'd been on the mound for what could have been two "finals" was meaningful. But as we hoped to keep our season alive our 7-3 victory sent our Bellmore Angels into a new round of games against another opponent up in upstate, New York.

I'd always learned to not to think too far ahead, the age old advice to take the games one at a time etched in my mind forever. I knew if we'd won in this round we'd be invited to Syracuse and then on to Battle Creek to play in the Stan Musial League World Series— the same place Thurman's Seran Agency team won it all when he was just 17. I wasn't getting ahead of myself but I sure did envision playing on the same field Thurman had played on, sitting on the same bench in the dugout he'd sat in, that sort of thing. I knew I'd feel a certain energy from such a thing, an energy that hadn't displaced itself, one that remained there forever. I wanted to go to Battle Creek for that.

A grueling five game schedule over two days and some of the worst umpire calls I'd ever been part of took away that dream. I'm not one who usually— if ever— places blame on an umpire, but this time a reversed decision— that included the local mayor getting involved— really made the difference in who was moving on and who was going home. I won't belabor the story, but suffice it to say it led to me being kicked out of the game, with all the drama and all the yelling going on following his brutal call sending me and two teammates to an early shower.

When he told me I didn't have my best stuff pitching that day I said, "Neither did you." When he asked me what I meant I said, "Because you overturned your call from the pressure the mayor put on you to do so." I guess that was enough for him to have heard from me, but to have your season end in such a way was painful and stayed with me for years.

But the pain was all part of the deal one makes with the game of baseball, that sometimes reaching a dream and other times experiencing a nightmare is separated by the thinnest of margins. And when you play long enough just about every player experiences both. And I knew, despite that nightmare produced from that one umpires call, that I wouldn't let it take me down, or sour me because of it. I was in it for the dreams.

It was no more than a year later when the movie, *Field of Dreams* was released to theaters, and in an instant, it became my favorite baseball movie of all time. It wasn't just the pure entertainment value and utter joy *Field* brought me, it became my favorite for other very personal reasons that I'm still emotional about, even today. Its many human attributes of courage, faith hope and self-sacrifice resonated in me along with those three magical whispered words, *Go The Distance* that sent a chill up my spine, almost as if they'd been meant for me.

I remember actually looking around the theatre when those words were first said, looking around for its source. I was so mesmerized and so focused on the screen, as those three whispered words were said a few more times, I really felt its strength— sort of like a sign— calling out to me in a way I find hard to describe.

To see the reaction on Ray Kinsella's face (Kevin Costner) when *go the distance* was first whispered as he looked around his cornfield before sitting down with a mostly confused and weary Terrence Mann (James Earl Jones), beaten down by life, not understanding what was going on and wondering what any of it had to do with him and why he was caught up in the whole mess. And when Ray witnessed an odd message flashing across the Fenway Park scoreboard about some, "Moonlight" Graham, (Burt Lancaster), that strong sensation I'd experienced when *Go the Distance* was spoken felt just as strong to me.

I'd had my share of experiences with an "inner voice" before, and as time went on, I learned to pay attention to it attracting *my attention*.

When I was 11 in 1974 playing my second year of Little League for the Indians, my friend and teammate Cory Teason was batting when I noticed how close their third baseman— John Lapi—was playing the batter. I tuned to our catcher Doug Vernet and said, "Next pitch Corey's gonna rip one off of Lapi's face," and just like that it happened on the very next pitch. Right after that Doug turned to me and said, "You're sick. I'm outta' here!" When I was 16 or 17 about 12 of us decided to grab some beers and sneak behind a school we'd never gone to before, an unusual spot to have chosen to chug down a few beers together and hopefully to not get caught.

That inner voice came over me just then, and I asked one of my buddies, "What would you do if a cop jumped that fence right there?" And he said, "I'd run, of course." No sooner did I point when a police officer hopped the fence running towards us, and my buddy sprinted off like a track star, the punishment for the rest of us the spilling out of any remaining beer we had and on our way we went.

In 1984 I was sitting on our couch with Suzette watching a playoff game between the Padres and Cubs when Steve Garvey stepped to the plate with hard-throwing Lee Smith on the mound. Out of nowhere that inner voice got my attention, I looked at Suzette and said, "Home run... right field," then boom, next pitch it happened—right down the line in right. Suzette just looked at me and said, "Wow!"

Of course the out-of-body experience I had after my headfirst fall was another in a string of "unexplainable" occurrences for me. And as that nudging from an inner-voice became more prevalent, I accepted it— even welcomed it— giving no thought to when it may come next or would ever come again.

I just knew I needed to pay attention to that inner-voice, that it was somehow connected to my journey, even having *the same birthday* as Kevin Costner, identifying strongly with Dwier Brown's portrayal of Costner's (Kinsella's) father John at the end of the movie and being utterly awakened by *Go The Distance* and *"Moonlight" Graham*. I couldn't wait to see where it all might go.

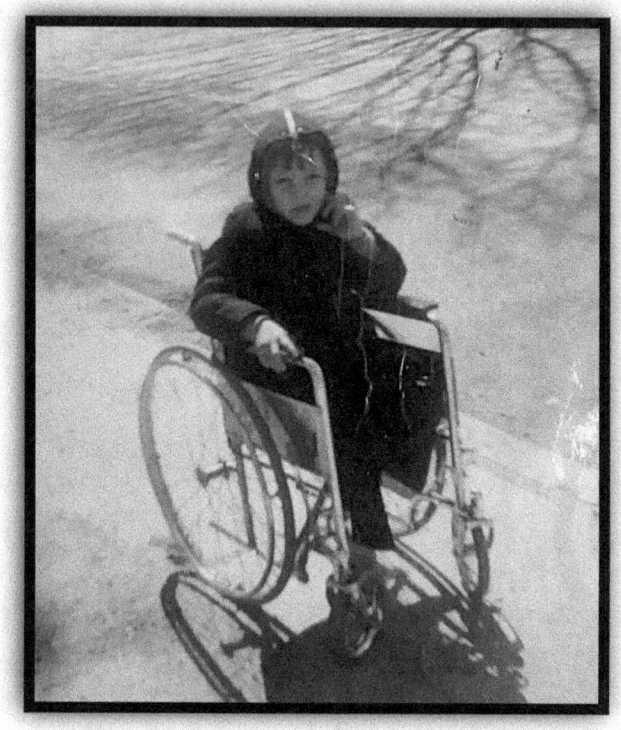

After spending a year bedridden, wheelchair bound in front of our house on Long Island.

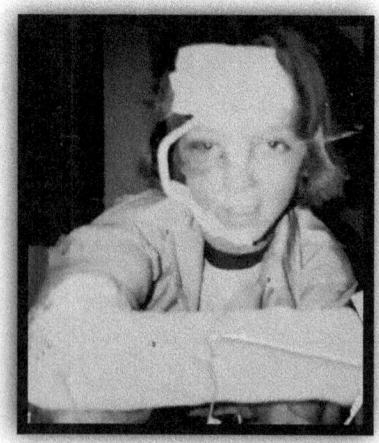

After falling at Winthrop Elementary School. Thankful to be alive. Sleeping with the game ball after pitching our only win of the 1973 season against the Yankees

1974 (L-R) with Phil Drago, myself, Tommy Cespites and Michael Cespites.

Before my diagnosis, I was the fastest kid around. Probably still am. That's me on crutches with brother Tim (far left), mom and Jimmy Donachie.

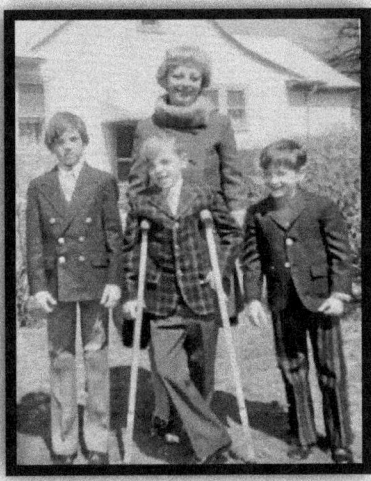

The first Munson Hall of Fame Committee is born at the 2019 Munson Awards Dinner. (L-R) Tom & Suzette Tunison, Adrienne Statfeld and Larry Schnapf.

(L-R): At the AHRC Dinner: Suzette with Kelly Munson: That's me with Diana Munson, and together with the amazing Thurman Munson supporter, Adrienne Statfeld.

We're a big baseball family and here's the pictures to prove it: Senior Day at Misericordia with son Jimmy and Suzette.

Like father, like son: Tommy bringing the heat for the Bath Haverling Rams in 2003 and me on the right, pitching for the Angels in 1986. Down below is Danny with Larry & Brenda after winning the MAAC championship with LeMoyne in 2007.

Four good buddies on the field and at a restaurant in Binghamton, moments before and after the Hall of Fame announcement: (L-R): Lou Rivera, Tom Tunison, Gary Kaschak, Marc Gambino.

(L-R):Together with Rene LeRoux and Gary Kaschak at the entrance to the Hall of Fame, moments before receiving my Thurman Munson autographed baseball. The day Thurman made the ballot, Cooperstown, 2019: (L-R): Mario Rivera, Jr., myself, Gary Kaschak and Marc Gambino

Bottom Left: Standing with Gary outside the entrance to the Hall of Fame: Bottom Right: Meeting Dwier Brown at Batavia Downs. One of the turning points to my story.

Church and music are a big part of my life. That's me on the left with Praise Band members Kirk Mishrell over my shoulder, Carolyn Jones to my side, and Gordon Vonderlin, Jim Robinson and Bob Mesler rounding out the band.

Gordon playing the drums. What a gifted drummer and talent he was. Rest in Peace, buddy. We miss you.

Top: Our growing family, Christmas, 2021
Middle Left: Walking Tara down the aisle, 2013
Middle Right: With brother Roy at Mossy Bank and campaigning for Thurman with my brother Bob at Yankee Stadium.

(L): With long time battery-mate and good friend Craig Stapleton, celebrating the induction of his mother, Mickey, into the New York State Baseball Hall of Fame. Our first female player to be inducted. (R): That's me and Craig with another good friend, (middle) Rob Esposito, continuing the celebration.

One of the biggest days of my life was not only meeting the Munson family, but sitting with them at their table at the AHRC Dinner, 2013. Some of my pride and joys: Two Thurman Munson baseball cards and co-authoring, "Thurman Munson's Decade of Unmatched Excellence," with Christopher Hahn.

Our last family photo: Top Row L-R: Bob, myself, Roy and Tim.
Bottom Row L-R: Deb, Mom, Ginnie and Lori

Mom & Dad just married. They would have been proud.

On snow-covered NYSEG Stadium in Binghamton, this photo was taken moments before the Hall of Fame announcement was made. Four of us stood in that same spot for photographs and only this one produced that beam of light. I'm sure some camera expert can give a rational explanation for this, but I take it as a sign...

Chapter 12
The Last Game

"Sure, my tryout for the Elmira Pioneers was far different than that of a player ever so close to batting in the major leagues, but nevertheless, it wasn't for me. I felt it. Go The Distance was in my ear."

By the summer of 1996 our lives were in constant movement. With Jimmy just turning two, Danny eight and Tommy 12, three boys kept us busy, and we made sure they had plenty to do with sports.

And we wanted it that way. From the very start of our marriage we'd talked about keeping any kids we'd have involved academically and in sports and to teach them the ropes of sports we were familiar with and to let them decide where they'd go with it. Of course baseball was my sport and always was and was easy for me to introduce the game to the boys and that's what I did first.

So I began coaching Tommy in T-Ball when he was six, and when he was ready for the minors I began coaching Danny in T-Ball. I had a huge calendar to write down everything going on during the baseball season, and I used colored markers as a guide. With the baseball season stretching four months, practice or a game every night, there was never a dull moment.

My flooring business became well-established by then, breaking the magic number of 10 years in business with a growing customer base and an excellent reputation. That combination allowed me flexibility with scheduling to coach the boys during those years— something I am is grateful for to this day.

But as much as I loved coaching and teaching baseball to the boys and their teammates, the urge to keep playing was always in the back of my mind. It had already been seven years since I hung up my spikes after playing semi-pro for five seasons when we lived on Long Island. But that urge to play just never left me. The fact that we started our family early certainly factored into my leaving the game when I did, but that urge, *that urge,* was building inside me. I really missed the competition and playing the game.

I'd heard about an adult hardball league that had started up in the area— the *Stan Musial League* that was similar to the level of competition I was used to being part of all those years. I'd kept myself in great shape over the years, due in part to the rigors of the business and good sense with diet and exercise, and at 32 years old was still in my prime. I'd told my boys stories of when I played and some of the games I'd been part of, and I felt they looked at me the same way I looked at all my baseball heroes. But my heroes had long retired or had passed away and the boys could only imagine stories I'd told them about the greats of the game— namely Thurman Munson.

Of course I'd told them all about Thurman. And there was no need to exaggerate or embellish anything he had done. They were old enough to know who my *heroes* were— *who my hero was and still is.* And as I told my Thurman Munson stories I decided to get back in the game to see if I still had it and to try and make the team. Thinking about Thurman Munson and talking about Thurman Munson always seemed to do something to me. It triggered something inside of me as if I had to do something— almost compelled to do something. It was a gnawing sensation that had gone dormant but had been building for a while. I couldn't explain it, that was for sure. But as the old memories of Thurman Munson flooded my mind, I went with my gut and decided to tryout for the team.

By the time I contacted the local team representing Bath, I was told it was too late. The roster has been set with a mixture of former college players, younger players and veterans with great baseball resumes. Feeling a bit dejected and taking it as a sign, still I felt downhearted and wished I had contacted the team earlier.

But the Bath coach gave me the contact name for the Corning team and told me they'd still been looking for players. He said that team would be merging players from Corning and Elmira and a few tryouts remained. In no time at all I made contact with the coach, Dan Fry, and drove 45 minutes to the tryout.

All along I just wanted to be one of the guys, not *The guy* that carried the load, or be the go-to player or star of the team. In a sense I was testing myself to see if I still had it, to see if the layoff had been too long and my skills had eroded to the point that I'd be finished. I felt like I still had it and could contribute, but none of that mattered now. I had to tryout and prove myself again. Turns out I was right about myself. Tryouts went well— exceptionally well. Not only did I make the team, but I made it as their number one starting pitcher and batted at the top of the lineup. At 32 years old I was back in the game!

Jay Maslyn was one of my Little League assistant coaches and when I told him I'd made the team he asked if there was room for one more player, that he wanted to tryout for the team. When they agreed it turned out to be a good thing because he could *play ball,* a real solid hitter and a raw student of the game. Together it turned out we were the two main cogs on the team.

The season went into the fall and the United States Rider Cup golf team from 95' was playing in Rochester that same day we were scheduled to play my hometown Bath team—the best team in the league. I'd been penciled in to pitch but when Jay told me he got tickets to see the Rider Cup team play in Rochester, I was terribly disappointed. I knew our chances of winning weren't very good, but without Jay— even for that one game— those odds dropped considerably. Needless to say we didn't do so well. I held on and struggled for four innings but we were clearly outnumbered and outplayed by a superior opponent. I wasn't too happy with Jay and I let him know in no uncertain terms how much I missed him— how much the team missed him— and that was that— over and done with. But we did have a lot of fun that season and decided to play again the following year. We'd won a few games and felt pretty good about ourselves as players.

I landed a carpet job in Elmira and read in the local paper that the Elmira Pioneers of the New York/Penn League were having open tryouts the same two days I was scheduled to lay carpet. Reading the article took me back in time when Thurman played in the same league and on Dunn Field for his first pro game— the very field where tryouts would be hosted. The irony played on my mind and the dreamer in me went to work again.

It had been 15 years since I'd tried out for the Yankees in Yankee Stadium and all those memories came back. I was stronger now and confident in what I could do and as I read the article again I decided to bring my uniform to work with me then head on down to Dunn Field for a tryout.

It was a short ride over to Dunn Field from the location I'd worked that day and when I walked into the stadium I still had my tool-pouch on, looking nothing like a ballplayer should. Grounds crews seemed to be everywhere but there was no sign of other players. I just walked right into the stadium when a friendly man approached me and asked if he could help me. I told him I was there for the tryout and he told me I was a day early, that tryouts were tomorrow and the next day and to come back tomorrow.

The job I had was for two days but I'd already completed half the work. Of course I was disappointed but remained excited and optimistic, and wondered how in the world I'd be able to come back for that second day tryout— if they even wanted me to. I hadn't even told my wife about it so I decided to take one day at a time and showed up the following day after work.

The first person I ran into was Ken Oberkfell, the new manager for the Pioneers and the old infielder for the Cardinals. I was carrying my uniform, and he asked me to follow him into the locker room. He didn't flinch or say very much, handed me a form to fill out and said to meet him on the field after the paperwork was completed. He put the form down and walked onto the field. It was a pretty standard form. Liability and injury waiver, name and address, that sort of thing. Then I hesitated at *Date of* Birth.

I was 33 years old at the time but looked far younger than that. I started filling in the date but wondered what they'd think about a 33 year old trying out for the team. I knew most of the guys in the league were in their early to mid 20's and if Oberkfell came back in and took a good look there'd be a good chance he'd ask me to leave.

So I starting forging my own license, changing the "3" into an "8" instantly taking five years off my life! I told myself I had to do it! I was about to finish when Oberkfell came back in said, "Let's get going, finish the paperwork later." He seemed real anxious to get me onto the field, so I dropped my pen before I could finish my "white lie" and left it on his desk.

I followed him out and started playing catch with a left hander I'd never meet who could really bring it. He was stocky and all business and seemed intent on making sure they'd notice him. I played ball for many year against college players and former pro players, but this kid was throwing hard. I held my own with him but that ball was moving pretty good.

So everybody did their job getting loose and soon enough they split the squads up only I was sent to the bench with a handful of other players. There were only about 20 players in total but I didn't like being one of those on the bench. I'd always been a starter and never a reserve, so it was an odd feeling as the scrimmage began.

At one point Oberkfell asked me if I was from the area and I said I wasn't and he said he could tell. Paul Blair was his assistant coach, and he was joking and being his jovial self trying to keep us loose and focused as we waited to hear our name called to enter the game. Oberkfell substituted after an inning or two and in the third inning he said suddenly, "Why don't you play some outfield. Can you take left field?"

Being an infielder and pitcher by trade, the outfield was the last place I wanted to play. I'd played outfield years ago but it certainly wasn't my strength. But what could I do? I told him left field was fine.

To this day I don't know why I never asked Paul Blair what it was like being a Yankee- and to play with Thurman Munson during the two Yankee World Series winning years— the only two years Blair was a Yankee. I was that close to talking with someone who knew Thurman Munson, who played with him and could see firsthand what he was like, what I already knew but wanted confirmed. I wanted to tell him about my relationship with Thurman, how I'd been bedridden watching Yankee games— my whole story. But I didn't want his pity, and thought better of it.

The next inning I ran out to left and was in absolute awe knowing I was in Dunn Field trying out for a professional baseball team. But that feeling didn't last long. The second or third batter drilled one over my head— a hard liner I knew would stay in the park and probably clank off the high wall behind me. I could not have played it any better. I took two steps and waited for the carom and it bounced on one hop right to me. I was determined to get the guy going into second base but the cutoff man was screaming at me.

Of course I hit the cutoff man, probably doing the right thing by showing them I understood some basic baseball fundamentals. But this was a tryout. It was the time to show off my arm, to show them what I had. I knew darn well I had a good shot at the guy at second base because I played it just perfectly. My one chance to shine was over. Another ball didn't come to me after that.

Several guys had to leave due to a few injuries so suddenly we didn't have a full fielding team. When Oberkfell told me I was going to pitch the next inning, I could hardly contain myself. I actually had reached that point where I'd be on the mound, that I pulled it off. It was really happening.

We didn't have a center fielder but we had a full infield. Our two outfielders were shaded towards the middle so I was at a big disadvantage as a pitcher. I pitched alright, recorded a couple quick outs then hung a curveball to one of the better prospects who smashed it off the wall just like the one that went over my head an inning earlier.

I didn't get the chance to get the third out. Ken called it a day right then. He said a few words to Paul Blair, and he announced who should report the next day and wished us well. And as he called my name to come back the next day, I smiled to myself I started packing my gear when the guy who hit one off the wall against me said he'd see me tomorrow. I took my uniform off, put my work clothes on and carried my gear to my car.

I'd finished my carpet job and another job in another town the next day was waiting for me but I couldn't do it. As much as I wanted to, I couldn't do it. I had a great job, a great wife, a growing family who needed me. I sought out the nearest pay phone I could find.

I called my wife and told her I just tried out for the Pioneers but didn't tell her they asked me back. She kiddingly asked me how much more money I was making, so kind and thoughtful in her approach—a friendly reminder that I was a dreamer— and maybe that was true. Maybe I was a dreamer.

About a month later I was getting ready to pitch against that same Bath team that whupped me the year before. There was an electrician working with me who knew all the Bath players, and he knew we were scheduled to play them the next week. I thought it over for a moment then said, "I have a message for them. Tell them I'm pitching that game and they're going down."

He looked surprised and said, "Really? And I said, "Really. You tell them that."

I had never said anything remotely like that before. I knew to never give an opponent any extra incentive, that they'd get all fired up and focus more than they usually had. They may have even decided to brush me back with a pitch or two, or even beaned me with one. But as I thought about all that, I was satisfied with what I said, supremely confident in my ability and wanting nothing more than to show them—to prove to them— that they wouldn't beat me and I wasn't kidding around.

I pitched that game against Bath, and this time Jay was there as our shortstop. I batted leadoff, cracked a pair of doubles, drew the only walk of the game and went the distance on the mound, inducing 14 popups in our enormously satisfying five hit, 3-1 victory.

There was quite a celebration afterwards, but I had so many mixed emotions of that week and not my baseball playing career. And as I reviewed that game later that night, I decided that would be the last game I'd ever pitch. Earlier in that game, my friend, Mickey Hubbard, lined one back at me on the mound that lightninged past my face and into centerfield—coming that close to seriously injuring me or even killing me. It was hit so hard it was by me before I could get my glove up.

I gave it a fleeting thought at the time, that I had a family and couldn't risk such things anymore, that a few inches separated me from disaster. But

I knew I had to finish the game, that I couldn't even think about leaving the mound after that. I said a silent prayer asking for protection and finished the job.

I played in one more game a week later in which my friend and teammate, Brian Hill, was within an inning of pitching a complete game when our coach came out to the mound for a conference with Brian, our catcher and the rest of our infielders. He took the ball from Brian and said, "Tom, you pitch the last inning."

I looked at my teammates and my coach and when I said, "No coach. I'm not gonna," he said, "What do you mean, you're not gonna?"

I had never been a disagreeable player or a rabble-rouser or insubordinate to any coach before, and I could tell that he could sense something was at play here—I could tell by that look in this eye. I said, "Let Brian finish the game. He's pitched a gem. He'll be fine." Coach looked at Brian, asked him what he thought and Brian said, "Give me the ball."

I tripled down the right field line in my last at bat during Brian's complete game victory— and I never played another game again.

When that week began I had no idea what decisions I was about to make, that I was about to walk away from baseball. And as I contemplated all that, I wish to this day I had gone back to that second tryout, to see if I really had what it takes, to sign even a one-day contract, to imagine a story being written of "Local Man Makes Team," to get my moment in the sun. That's all I ever wanted.

We attended a Pioneers game a few weeks later, but I didn't recognize any of the players on the field from those I'd tried out with that day— and as I imagined myself as *that one* who could have been there, Manager Ken Oberkfell recognized me in the stands and tipped his cap to me.

As Oberkfell tipped his cap to me, I thought about what I'd learned some time ago that "Moonlight" Graham was an actual major league ball player, that his portrayal of Dr. Archibald Graham in *Field Of Dreams* had been the truth, and while he played in just one game for the Giants in 1905, he never came to bat. But an addition fact— the date that "Moonlight"

Graham's one game played was the exact same date— June 29th— as my Yankee tryout was.

I thought about that the second Ken Oberkfell acknowledged me, and felt that connection I'd felt to "Moonlight" Graham grow stronger. Sure, my tryout for the Elmira Pioneers was far different than that of a player ever so close to batting in the major leagues but nevertheless, it wasn't for me. I felt it. *Go The Distance* was in my ear.

Chapter 13
Beware The Fury

"Amongst the chatter of sharing our fortune cookie messages with each other, mine really spoke to me. Really spoke to me. It read, Beware the fury of a patient man."

There was quite a lengthy gap in my life when I had no time to take any ideas or concerns I may have had regarding Thurman Munson. In fact, those dormant years started as far back as 1985 and stretched all the way into 2010.

But I always liked to dream and dream big. There was always something gnawing at me but so many distractions made those dreams seem so distant to me. I'd entertained some ideas every now and then, wanted to get back in to my research for Thurman Munson, but raising a family, working for myself and trying to save for the future was far more important than developing any dreams or ideas I might have had. And while so much time had passed since I'd first watched *Field of Dreams,* I never gave up hope on any of its messages I'd taken personally.

I hadn't lost sight of the fact that Thurman's final year of Hall of Fame eligibility had come in 1995, but by then I'd virtually lost all hope in the voting process and in those who'd been responsible for the voting.

Sure, Thurman had been on the ballot for all 15 years of eligibility— something that hardly ever happens for any eligible player— but the voting numbers told the story. Following his first year of eligibility when he received over 15% of the vote, the following years dropped off mostly into single digits, another bad sign for his chances.

I'd continued following the voting path of other players who'd been voted in, and noticed the same pattern I'd spotted 15 years earlier and knew deep down— despite my optimistic nature— that Thurman had virtually no chance. I certainly hoped the voters would have paid attention to that fact and recognize the time was now or never but it was unrealistic to think that way. And I was right. When the votes were tabulated, Thurman received a paltry 6.5% and I knew what that meant. He was off the ballot for good, kicked to the curb to join other greats of the game deserving a far better fate.

I was disgusted at the results as I usually was *really disgusted.* How was it that these so called baseball experts had missed all the great things Thurman had accomplished? He was a Rookie of The Year, an MVP, won all those Gold Gloves, had been voted or chosen onto all those all-star teams, won two World Series championships and was a Yankee captain. It was a combination of anger, disgust, and a bit of helplessness I was feeling. Anger at the system, disgust at the voters and helplessness because I still— after all these years—didn't know what to do, didn't know how I could help from afar. I felt so powerless and wanted things to change.

I had to pin my hopes now on the Veterans Committee, the voting arm of baseball that recognizes players like Thurman and others who needed their help. Certainly they'd come to their senses and acknowledge the obvious oversight others had made on Thurman Munson for 15 straight years. This would be their chance to right a wrong that had festered for 15 years. And that meant more waiting, more wondering and likely more disgust.

But as the years flew by, Thurman's name wasn't called. By 2000, contemporaries like Jim Bunning, Nellie Fox, Orlando Cepeda and Bill Mazeroski were chosen by the Veterans, but nothing for Thurman. And by 2010, when no other player from Thurman's era was elected by the Veterans, I had grown completely tired of the voting politics for the Hall of Fame.

I'd waited year after year to hear Thurman's name announced, but it never was. It was a hollow, empty feeling, and I could see the writing on the wall for each and every vote. But I wouldn't allow what had happened bring me down— ever.

They say hope springs eternal, and I wasn't about to give up. It's in my nature and always has been. I was that same kid who raised himself up from a bed, from his wheelchair and from his crutches. There was no way in the world I would abandon any hope for Thurman's induction. I felt like I owed it to him to try and figure out something I could do for him, that I was the only one in his corner. He was my hero, and I wasn't giving up.

It was late Fall during that 2010 year when another awakening happened for me, another epiphany. A life-changing event from something so very simple, something many people never would have recognized as another sign. But I've learned over the course of my life that's how it all works. That if you leave yourself open to interpreting everything happening around you, that sometimes there are signs left for us to use or discard, not all the time, but at just the right time. What better way for the course of my life to change than through a good old Chinese fortune cookie.

We had ordered takeout from Ling Ling, a local Chinese restaurant where we lived in Bath. As usual, we all opened our fortune cookies and I read mine once, then again and again. Amongst the chatter of sharing our fortune cookie messages with each other, mine really spoke to me. Really spoke to me. It read, Beware the fury of a patient man.

I remember thinking it sounded like a message for a madman, but I thought about it further. That was not it at all. I began too think that I could have fury inside but could internalize it while being smart at the same time. Earlier that day I had argued with people on the internet about Thurman Munson, doing my best to present the facts about Thurman and the case I was building for the Hall of Fame.

Up to that point I was an old-school guy regarding baseball statistics like batting average, home runs and runs batted in. New metrics, like WAR and OPS+ had made inroads to the baseball world, but I hadn't taken much of it very seriously. But I knew deep down that I'd have to change my attitude and learn the new metrics, to be able to incorporate them into defending and presenting Thurman Munson more thoroughly and intelligently. That I'd argued with others earlier who'd had a better understanding of the new numbers got me thinking. Beware the fury of a patient man would become my mantra. I'd learn and embrace the new metrics in due time. I folded the little white strip of paper the saying came in and placed it into my wallet. And all these years later, there it stays today, a constant reminder for me to stay patient and strong. I still pulled that little strip of paper out at appropriate times when things were tough and I read it to myself. And every time I read the words it took me back to the voters who'd overlooked Thurman and reminded me I had to do something about it.

All the while I was scheming and dreaming and concocting some kind of plan, I started researching the statistics of hundreds of players who I believed should have already been inducted into Cooperstown that began with Thurman Munson. And although I had promised myself to learn the new metrics of baseball, I started with the old school statistics I'd learned as a kid, of batting average, home runs and runs batted in for batters, and wins, losses, earned run average, strikeouts and saves for pitchers.

I played with the numbers constantly, comparing and contrasting statistics to those in the Hall of Fame, trying to make sense of the formula I was inventing. I wanted to know why some players were in the Hall and others with better or equal numbers were not. I wanted to create a fair and equitable formula that made sense, one that had an obvious degree of difficulty in its outline. I wanted to set the bar in such a way that it made not only mathematical sense to me, but to baseball in general. I wanted to share my findings with the baseball world, to let them to know there just might be a better way to evaluate a player and his career. That's when I had an epiphany. I'd create my own version of the Hall Of Fame, The American Baseball Honors Academy.

After months of calculations, cross-outs, scribbles and notes, the crunching of numbers I had dutifully and meticulously calculated began making perfect sense to me. I had fact-checked every number on every player dozens of times, made appropriate changes to any formula that was made and felt an exhilarating confidence in what I'd prepared. I was so convinced in the numbers and the concept of creating another brick and mortar location similar to Cooperstown's, that I could envision the whole thing in my mind, and knew that if I was really serious and it wasn't just a fantasy, I had to get the ball rolling by asking others to help and advice.

Danny Kouw was a friend of mine and a graphic artist who made posters promoting the Academy. I sat down with a lawyer and discussed opening the museum in a brick-and-mortar location somewhere in Western New York State. And on August 2, 2010, I wrote the following letter in hopes of attracting fans.

"Time! The corrector when our judgments err."- Lord Byron

It has been 31 years since Thurman Munson's tragic death. I was 16 years old at the time and I was certain then just as I am now that he was a very, very special baseball player.

As a boy I delivered newspapers in the town of Bellmore, New York, some 30 miles from New York City and Yankee Stadium, the home of my baseball heroes. I read the stories, watched the games and collected the players baseball cards as well. I poured over the stats on the cards backside. I would wait in anticipation for the league leaders to be posted in the newspapers, which was usually once a week, to see who was leading their respected league in the all important categories of batting average, runs batted in and home runs. From a very early age, I was for some reason fascinated with stories of the games past history and I could not seem to get enough of it. I followed the game as closely as anyone in my position possibly could, and I still do. I read all the sportswriters columns and appreciated the news they would bring me about my heroes. Thurman Munson may have rubbed some of them the wrong way. This is part of life and we all have to deal with it in our own way.

The writers have the power. They decide in their own words what we get to read. They give us their opinions and then decide on who goes to the Baseball Hall of Fame. They decide. I am tired of this old and worn out formula. Why are so many of the games great players being overlooked for induction? It has really become quite outrageous, and it is time for a change.

The Hall of Fame is a great place to visit and Cooperstown is a great little town to visit and enjoy. I think it is time to make it more enjoyable for more people. There are many players on the outside of this great museum looking in that should not be. Their numbers and their accomplishments are too easily overlooked. If the Hall of Fame was just based on numbers that had to be achieved in order for a player to be inducted, many of them would not have made it in. This is part of the problem. The writers get sentimental for some players and not for others. That is a rotten formula. If a player was a great player in his time then he should be recognized and remembered. That is why the Hall was created, to celebrate and enjoy the game and its great players.

In Thurman Munson's case, he was the best of his time. Time has only helped the case of this great player. Unfortunately for him, nobody is paying attention to the details. There are only four players in the games history to have won a Rookie of the Year Award, a league Most Valuable Player Award and at least two World Series championships in their career. They are Frank Robinson, Johnny Bench, Pete Rose and Thurman Munson.

During the decade of the 1970's, baseball great Rod Carew had eight seasons in the American League that he batted .300 or better. Thurman Munson is next on the list with five seasons. In his last full season of 1978, Munson fell two hits shy of making it six seasons. That is pretty amazing stuff for a guy who caught at least 130 games for seven straight years from 1972 through 1978, making him one of only six catchers in the games history to do so. The other catchers to accomplish this are Yogi Berra, Johnny Bench, Jim Sundberg, Jorge Posada and Jason Kendall. This includes postseason games which is another place where Thurman Munson excelled. He holds the record for best batting average ever for catchers in postseason and playoff games with at least 50 at bats. He also hold the record for the best batting average ever for catchers in World Series games with at least 50 at bats at .373. There is not one catcher who even comes close to his World Series record. This is the time of year where catchers are worn down and hitting becomes extremely difficult. Why has baseball not celebrated this? I think I know why and I have stated it above.

I have a lot more information to share with you on Thurman Munson but who do I tell? Who will listen and who will get the word out? Munson is one of the many who deserve recognition for their achievements. Wouldn't it be great if we had a place of our own to celebrate our heroes, a place where sportswriters don't tell us who belongs there, but we decide? It is about time that we the fans had the power to do some decision making of our own, and it is my dream to make that come true. I am inviting you to join me on this quest, and I am offering you a chance to be one of the decision makers! This is going to be a whole new ballgame, as the saying goes.

Please join me and help me create a new place, The Fans Museum, inspired by Thurman Munson. Who knows, maybe your hero could end up there as well- but then that would be up to you!

A few months later and carrying the excitement of its possibilities, I wrote a second letter. I had spent that two months digging into the stats of hundreds of players and was excited to announce the names of players who had qualified under the guidelines I'd established earlier.

So on September 28, 2010, I wrote this follow-up letter to the fans.

It has been nearly two months since I made the decision to create a new place for Baseball fans to come and celebrate the game while honoring the great players of the past 50 years. I have continued to research the players who qualify because of the outstanding numbers that they produced during their careers. It has been great fun revisiting the careers of these players.

At this point I have discovered six pitchers and 38 position players that qualify for the Highest Honors. Also at this point I have come across six pitchers and 42 position players that qualify for the Honor Roll. These men have achieved certain numbers during their playing days that make them stand out above the rest.

After meeting with Mr. Chris Wilkins in Victor, New York on September 20th, and receiving advice and support for my idea and how to move forward, I have decided on the name for the establishment. It will be called, The Baseball Fans Honors Academy.

Mr. Wilkins puts the cost of getting this project off the ground at somewhere about $75,000 for it to be successful with a top-notch website. I am anxious to proceed and will contact him soon.

The Academy will be a non-profit organization with myself as caretaker. The fans will have the final say as to who goes on the ballot when they pay a small fee to cast their vote. And this will be the highest honor bestowed on a player.

By October, I'd established the final criteria for induction into my academy, and by December I wrote, *"My wish to own our own facility— the Fans facility— has now become more important and more urgent. It is time to get the ball rolling. I am ready to bring this idea to the masses and I pray they embrace it."*

The shift in the paradigm was feeling so very real to me now. I would not allow outside influences to deter me from turning my dream into a reality. I would stay focused on moving forward, at all times keeping the memory of Thurman Munson alive and fueling my desire in giving him a proper place where fans could come and celebrate him. It may not have been Cooperstown, but it still mattered, and it mattered a lot to me.

I had envisioned lines of fans waiting to come into our facility. Families, couples, old-timers, you name it. I'd witnessed the looks on faces before while in Cooperstown at the Hall of Fame. The utter look of joy on the faces of old Brooklyn Dodgers fans, of Yankee fans, of Braves and Giants fans, and the Pirates and the Red Sox, the Cardinals and Phillies. Every team from every city.

And I'd felt the magic myself. My heroes displayed like Kings and treated like one. Reverence bestowed by awed fans of all ages, looking and studying game worn uniforms, bats, gloves, balls and caps, all of it in grand order and perfection, and remembering what it was like to be a kid again. Of course I'd always enjoyed Cooperstown because of my deep love for baseball. I'd shared many of the feelings of my fellow patrons to the Hall and left always with great respect and a sense of joy that is so hard to explain. Almost like a heaven on earth feeling.

But there was a void at the Hall and an emptiness I'd felt in the pit of my stomach. Thurman Munson was missing. Worse still, as I contemplated what I didn't want to admit, was the fact that he may never get in unless the voters came around to my way of thinking.

I penned a letter in January of 2011 to our local newspaper, *The Courier*, writing about my dismay with the Hall of Fame procedures and the injustices to many of the greats of the game who hadn't been inducted.

I touched upon my academy idea, citing numerous examples and ideas I had for it. I was pleased when that story, *Would Hall of Fame founders be pleased?* ran a few days later.

I was pleased that story ran and content that I'd finally put into motion my academy concept. I wasn't done by a long shot to what I wanted to do, and I knew deep down that something else would be coming down the pike. I knew I'd stay directly involved in campaigning for Thurman Munson until my final days. Perhaps my museum was the ticket, that I'd be the one banging the drum loudest, that I'd be the one going the distance for him.

Chapter 14
The Postcard

"But I knew better than that. My whole life had been a series of such feelings like this one, premonitions that came true. Dreams and thoughts that came true."

I was excited about the prospect of opening my Baseball Academy and moving things forward. I thought about it when I went to bed at night and I thought about it in the morning. I thought about it during the day and the cycle kept on repeating itself every day. I was consumed with taking the next steps to whatever it may have taken, but like everything else when a good idea is born, sometimes life just got in the way of the dream.

But it was all good. We had a growing family, and the time needed to properly develop the Academy wasn't there. There just wasn't enough hours in a day. I needed to support my family, that was and always has been my number one priority. I realized then that any extra hours I'd have during the course of a day, a week, a month, just didn't add up to what I knew was needed to get the Academy open. I had to shelve the idea for now.

Something else inside was telling me it was time for a change, and it had nothing to do with putting the Baseball Academy on hold. My mind was going off in other directions. I started entertaining the idea of leaving the flooring business and doing something else. After all, I'd spent 25 years in the flooring business and it was starting to takes its toll on my body. All the bending and kneeling and lifting came with a price, and in a strange sort of way, I had even more appreciation for the catching position in baseball, how the wear and tear from the constant kneeling and rising affects the body. And I was in great shape. I'd always taken good care of my body, so it had nothing to do with being overweight or anything physical. I just knew that at some point I'd probably have to change careers.

I'd think about Thurman from time to time when I squatted into position measuring or laying carpet on some floor. I imagined what it was like to be a catcher and to squat over like he did for all those innings. Just making that simple motion into the squatting position and back up gave me a real perspective of the rigors the position brings. And to add the weight of the catcher's gear, hot summer temperatures and everything else that went into catching really makes you think about how hard the position is and what it does to the body over time. There's no other position on the field like it and I wondered sometimes if any of the voters really understood what it takes and why it was that Thurman Munson had been overlooked the way he had been.

Even laying carpet Thurman was always in the back of my mind. It made me feel connected to Thurman in a most unusual way, especially at times when I was alone in the room and it was quiet or I was on a break. It really gave me time to reflect on my life and where it was headed— even to where Thurman's life may have been headed had he survived the accident. I looked forward to those moments by myself, thinking things out and sketching out the future for me and my family. As I was removing an old carpet at a residence in Hammondsport, New York, I discovered a faded newspaper dated August 3rd, 1979 with full coverage of Thurman Munson's death. As I leafed through its pages wondering how this could be, I nodded to myself knowingly. This was yet another sign from the universe and no coincidence at all.

But the future wasn't as easy to see as laying out carpet was. From measuring, cutting and installing, I always knew what to expect when it was over. Results were guaranteed in writing. Everything would fit as planned with hardly ever any surprises or errors. And if any error had been made, they were usually easy ones to fix. I found some irony in the whole thing. I'd carved out thousands of feet of carpet creating thousands of new paths for people's homes. Occasional mistakes had been made and corrected almost immediately. Changing careers would create a new path for me, one with more questions than answers and certainly no guarantees.

So I made the change, made another leap of faith and started working in the abstract business. It was something I had learned while working part-time during my flooring career, learning property title searches, judgement claims, that sort of thing. And with the oil and gas industry booming just 20 miles away in northern Pennsylvania, that little bit of experience I gained was enough to land me a great job. For me, it was just another example of how the life path that had been created for me connected perfectly all these years later. I had no idea when I'd learned the abstract field that one day it would launch another career. To my way of thinking, it was planned out from some higher force and I'd recognized that. I was eager to see where it was headed.

That decision to change careers was the right one. I loved what I was doing and held an important position with my company, grateful for what had happened and how I felt about things. The fact that the nearly three hour round trip drive back and forth every day wasn't the perfect setup, it gave me some alone time to listen to music, sports or simply to reflect some more.

I'd noticed a little antique store during the ride home and began stopping in to break up the monotony from the drive and curious to look around. I love old antiques and in particular old baseball stuff, so it was something to look forward to. The store was really intimate with tight aisles. They seemed to have plenty of merchandise with a lot of variety, but I was always drawn to a section where postcards were displayed on a card rack. My sister Ginnie loves old postcards, so I'd buy a few for her from time to time just to make her happy and put a smile on her face. I think I got a few items for myself from that store, then suddenly, I just lost the desire to go in anymore. It wasn't because of poor service or anything like that. In fact, the woman who owned the store was always pleasant and engaging. It was probably a combination of being tired and just wanting to get home. I just don't remember why I stopped going.

Months later during the drive home a sudden urge to pull into the parking lot and go into the antique store overcame me. It was a strong feeling I kept having but I was really tired that night just wanting to get home and relax a bit. As I came within a mile or two of the antique store, that nagging thought grew stronger. I really was tired and made the excuse to myself that I didn't have the time to stop, that the urge to get home was greater than listening to some voice in my head.

But I knew better than that. My whole life had been a series of such feelings like this one, premonitions that came true. Dreams and thoughts that came true. And as my tired mind contemplated this latest message, I was pulled back to the day in 1984 when Steve Garvey batted against Hall of Fame pitcher Lee Smith in the playoffs, when I announced to my wife confidently and succinctly, "Next pitch, home run, dead- right field." And just like that, the right-handed, pull hitting Garvey planted the next pitch from the hard-throwing, right- handed Smith into the right field seats—dead right field. That I'd gone out on a limb to call that pitch perfectly correct didn't feel so special to me. I'd heard the voice tell me to make the call, and had trusted it before.

Or during a title search in 2003, when the name, *Livingston* appeared during the investigation, reminding me of grade school childhood friend Scott Livingston and all the great times we shared together. That we hadn't been in contact with each other for nearly 30 years. How within the hour my cell phone rings and the voice on the other end is none other than Scott Livingston.

Or the time I carpeted a bedroom for a woman three years earlier when we still lived on Long Island. How suddenly the thought of her and the directions she'd given me to her house came to mind. How that route to her house stayed with me the entire day and how I'd not been in contact with her since the project was completed. And then that night she called me at home, asking if I could install another carpet for her.

As I thought about all this and what *Thurman Munson postcard* could possibly mean, I pulled onto the little dirt path leading to the store parking lot and went inside. I just had to. I said hello to the owner, and we talked for a while. She asked why I hadn't been by for such a long time and I told her I'd been busy, that sort of thing.

But I was really anxious to get back to the postcard section at the back of the store. *Thurman Munson postcard* kept repeating itself in my mind. And as I walked down a few aisles towards the postcard section, something else told me to turn around and go back to the counter. I followed that instruction until I arrived at another counter when I spotted a 1971 Thurman Munson postcard displayed. I said to myself, "You've got to be kidding me."

It wasn't just that a Thurman Munson postcard suddenly appeared, or that the voice directing me to the store had my attention, it was thinking back to the 1971 Topps baseball cards— my favorite set of all. And that 71' set had my favorite card of Thurman Munson, the one with the black border. I remembered, amazingly, how I kept getting that Munson card in just about every pack of cards I bought. I remembered taking a thin rubber band and putting them around my favorite cards, then a thicker rubber band I used for cards I didn't care so much about, the ones that would take more of a beating. But those Munson cards with the thin runner band I took care of, putting them in shoe boxes like everybody did. I hadn't forgotten that years later my mom gave them all away to my cousin's daughter and how I wish I had them back. And now, all these years later, standing alone in a little antique store, staring at the image of my hero on a postcard, I was feeling blessed.

As I fixated on the Thurman Munson postcard I hadn't yet noticed the others. Roy White, Fritz Peterson, Ralph Houk and others all seemed to be in great shape, beautiful shape. I was pretty sure I'd seen the set before online and wanted to buy them all, on the spot. And as I opened my wallet to see how much cash I had, I said in Rizzuto-like fashion, "Holy cow... what are you asking for these postcards?" "Thirty dollars," she replied. I counted my cash. Five dollars.

I knew she hadn't accepted credit cards and told her my dilemma and how badly I wanted the Munson card—how I needed the Munson card— even how I was drawn into her store that night. She mentioned that the collection was for sale as a set, that she wasn't interested in selling each card by itself. I took more time explaining what Thurman had meant to me in my life and that was the reason I was there. I offered $2.50 for the Munson card and another $2.50 for Houk's. She eyed me over and said, "Alright. Five dollars for the two."

I really loved Roy White and the other players, but for some reason I wanted to get Thurman's manager, Ralph Houk. I'm not sure why I hadn't asked her to hold the other cards for me, that I'd stop by another night on the way home from work to buy the rest, but I felt satisfied with the deal we'd made. I was floating for the remaining part of the drive home.

When I got home and told Suzette what had happened and shared my thoughts on the spirituality of what occurred, she agreed it was all part of some plan, that it was meant to be. It was the strongest of any premonition or vision I'd ever experienced. The fact that I was headed to the postcards and past the counter when I had the feeling I should turn around, just blows my mind. I didn't even have to thumb through the postcards, they were just sitting there waiting for me on the counter. I don't know how to explain it. I'm very spiritual believing in God and Jesus, and am guided by God in everything I do. I feel God can do anything he wants to do for us and through us. God uses people. I think God absolutely directed me to that store. He knows the value of baseball in my life and he knows what baseball has done for my life and how much Thurman means to me. God definitely guided me to the post cards. And it's continued the journey.

Chapter 15
Yankee Royalty

"We looked at each other and I said, "Diana Munson." And she said, "You're not gonna cry are you?"

As I thought about my role in all this, I'd been thinking about the Annual Munson Awards Dinner for the better part of a year, imagining myself attending *just one* in my lifetime, knowing without a doubt it would definitely be one of my biggest thrills.

But I was sure the price of tickets were out of our league for now. Maybe one day in the future, when my Baseball Academy was thriving, and the kids were older we'd be able to go to one. I'd always wanted to attend a Thurman Munson dinner and especially to have the chance to meet Diana Munson in person. Diana Munson was like Yankee Royalty to me— right up there with Mrs. Ruth and Mrs. Gehrig— Yankee ladies of the Yankee greats. When I was a kid and first learned the names of all those Yankee legends their wives would sometimes appear on the Yankees broadcast and it just blew me away. I remember thinking, "My gosh that's Babe Ruth's wife... that's Lou Gehrig's wife." And as I thought about those two ladies I wondered how I'd react if I ever met Thurman Munson's wife in person. I had goosebumps just thinking about it.

As I thought more about the dinner, I thought it would be the perfect gift for my 50th birthday. I knew that *The Big Five-O* should be celebrated differently than most others. After all, milestones have always meant a lot to me. I thought further that maybe there was a way we could save and cut back on a few other things, to scrape enough together to make it work, to be able to go to the dinner. That's when I told Suzette that I didn't want a big party.

I just didn't want to be the big focus of something like that, that what I'd love to do instead was to go to the Munson dinner. I told her it was the best way for me to get to meet Diana Munson and to tell her my feelings about Thurman, that it would probably be my best chance to spend a minute with her if I was to be that lucky. I knew that even if we went to the dinner there would be no guarantee I'd meet her, but I knew I'd do everything in my power to make it happen. Deep down, I really thought if we made it there, I'd connect with Diana Munson even for a moment or two.

That inner-voice kept talking to me, that same voice from all those other times, compelling me I needed to go, that it was *that* important. There's such a fine-line explaining this feeling I get sometimes, somewhere between wishful thinking and submission, with no grey area at all.

But that other side of me— one of reason and reality— was strong as well and played into it. I knew tickets were expensive but didn't really know how much they were and never looked into it. I dropped hints sometimes and hoped why wife would take the bait. And as the days and weeks flew by and my birthday approached, I was still hoping— and still hearing that inner-voice.

On the day of my birthday Suzette presented me an envelope and didn't say anything, just handed it to me. I could tell by the look on her face that this was something special, and I grinned knowingly. I opened it up *real slow* and pulled out its contents— and there it was in all its glory— an invitation to the Thurman Munson dinner. I just couldn't believe it. She did it.

As I beamed in absolute delight Suzette told me she'd been stashing some money for quite a while and had paid for two tickets in advance. She went on to explain why the tickets weren't in the envelope, that the rule was we'd have to pick tickets up on the day of the event at the door in person. I thought that to be a little odd but showed no concern or asked any questions, probably because my mind was so preoccupied on what just happened. Holy Cow! We were going to the dinner— that's what I knew—

and whatever the rules were was no problem as far as I was concerned. We'd get our tickets at the door like everybody else.

Our tickets would get us into the basic reception before the dinner, and that a second more private reception was where all the big whigs and the Thurman Munson Award recipients would gather for photographs and the like— an hour of seeing "who's who" in baseball as well as stars from other sports and the media. We'd be able to mix with a more general public before actual seating began.

As I gave it some thought I wished that maybe we'd get lucky and see one or two stars mingling in the lobby before they had to leave for the grand reception. Maybe I'd get lucky and Diana Munson would walk by and I'd get her ear for even a few seconds. I don't know, it was just wishful thinking on my part. I didn't know what the layout of the place was or anything like that, but still, I could think positive thoughts and say a few prayers.

This was mid-January in 2013, just a few weeks before the dinner and I was like a kid counting down the days. The calendar seemed to be moving at a snails pace and I felt so anxious and a bit nervous just thinking about everything. I even memorized a few words as to what I'd say to Diana if the chance came up. I wondered how far back our table would be from the main stage, who we'd be seated with and the rest of the details coming to mind. I hoped we'd be facing the stage and have a real good sightline for photos. But all that really didn't matter that much. I was so grateful to be going to the event, so grateful that I'd at least get a glimpse of Diana and be part of such a great night.

With the great countdown down to its last day, I wanted to make sure we'd make a good impression. I spent the morning washing and vacuuming the car and picked up my suit at the dry cleaners in the afternoon. I was really excited— like a kid at Christmas thinking about meeting Diana Munson—it was that big a deal for me.

It was about 300 miles from Bath to New York City giving us plenty of time to talk things over in the car. The ride was smooth all the way right into the city and being as familiar as I was we parked and were ready for the big event. We tipped the Parking attendant well, and that turned out to be a great move because when we came out at the end of the night our car was front and center. That final touch added to the perfection of the whole night.

We entered the Hyatt and noticed the table where people were checking in for the event. They asked our names and when we told them we were Tom and Suzette Tunison, a woman jumped up from the table, recognizing Suzette's name. She seemed overly excited to see her, and I was taken aback by the whole thing, thinking that was quite a greeting. Then another woman at the table said, "Tunison?" and I said yes. She handed me the tickets that had, *Table #1* written on it. It didn't dawn on me at the time that it was anything special. I don't know, there were so many distractions and I had so much going on in my head at that moment. I found out who the woman was as we started walking around the place, Suzette telling me she was the person who took her order over the phone and was happy to meet her in person.

We had about 30 minutes before the reception began and that's when Suzette let me in on a few more things. She told me she'd called for tickets a few months earlier and explained to Meredith— the woman she just hugged— that it needed to be a surprise, that I'd notice any unusual envelope when the mail came to our house. So they arranged for the letter with the tickets to have no tell-tale signs of where it was coming from— nothing that would tip me off. The plan worked like a charm. When the envelope arrived at our house I wasn't curious at all. A perfect plan it was.

I asked if we could go upstairs and was told that's where the dinner reception was being held and we weren't allowed in quite yet. I'd noticed earlier that the guest of honor reception room was downstairs and down the hall from where we were talking. She said we'd be allowed in shortly and she pointed to that very room. The entrance had been roped off, and the guard told me it was too early, so I started talking to him about Thurman and the Hall of Fame.

I had caught myself talking about Thurman to baseball fans and even total strangers all the time— that's how passionate I was about it. I'd take any opportunity— under the right circumstances— to say what I had to say— almost like some preacher standing on a soap box spreading the word. I felt pretty strong about that. You never know who's listening or who they might know. Keeping all that I knew about Thurman to myself wasn't doing him any good, and it made me feel stronger and more confident the more I talked about it. Being in New York around so many Yankee fans could really open up doors to conversation that started with this guy. I was pretty excited he'd listened and agreed with me, and I was anxious for more opportunities to repeat myself.

About 15 minutes later that same guard motioned to us from down the hallway as he detached the rope from the rail, actually allowing us to attend the big-whig reception! And as we walked in Dwight Gooden was standing right in front on us. I introduced ourselves and he took photos with us and signed a ball we brought from home. Then we met John Flaherty of the Yankees and Dave Phelps— a rookie pitcher about to receive the Thurman Munson Rookie Award. We met Greg Anthony of the NBA—a great announcer and terrific guy who signed his autograph and took pictures with us. The revolving-door of athletes kept coming—Ike Davis of the Mets— whose dad Ron played with Thurman. At this point I put two and two together and thought our ticket to *Table #1* meant we were part of the celebrity party after all.

Suzette and I had gone our separate ways for the better part of an hour, doubling our chances of meeting more celebrities. We'd meet up every few minutes to compare notes, and I asked her if she'd seen Diana Munson in the room, but she hadn't. Of course Diana had been the primary person I wanted to meet, and I was getting concerned neither of us had seen her yet.

The room was dimly lit and off to the side I noticed two women in conversation. I had a feeling the woman with her back to me was Diana and as I got up the courage to approach her, the other woman walked away.

I remember saying to myself there was no way this could be her standing alone in this room, but as she turned around *it was her* and I couldn't believe it. I couldn't believe I had her all to myself at that moment, what I'd been hoping for all along. And there she was, just the two of us. No line. No people.

We looked at each other and I said, "Diana Munson." And she said, "You're not gonna cry are you?" I said, "No. I'm not gonna cry." She said, "Can I give you a hug?" And I said, "Absolutely."

And there I was hugging Diana Munson. *Diana Munson!* I pulled back after a moment, looked at her and said in the most sincerest, reverent way I knew, "You have no idea what your husband meant to me. He was just an amazing ball player and since I was a kid I wanted to tell that to you face-to-face. He changed my life."

She said she gets that all the time, big old guys coming up to her crying and hugging her. She said, "Thank you so much for that." Suzette had been standing there the whole time, and she hugged her too. I was amazed that there we were—just the three of us—talking and sharing without interruption. It took about five minutes before others started coming around and she told us she had to go.

Suzette stopped her and said "Tom wanted you to signed Thurman's book," and I said, "No, I wanted her to sign this" and pulled out the postcard that was tucked inside the book. She took a look at his picture and said, "Oh my God, he was just a baby." I'm sure by her reaction she'd never seen that postcard and had a distant look in her eye. She took the postcard and a pen I'd brought, flipped it over and asked me my name and as she started writing I started crying. And then Suzette said, "Now he's crying." She signed, *"To Tom. Thank you for all your loyalty. Best Wishes. Diana Munson."* I was just blown away.

There I was standing with the postcard I had been called to by some inner-voice, the woman I just had to meet and my wife who made it all happen. And as I tried processing one of the most precious moments in my life, two of Diana's children— Thurman Munson's children— approached their mother.

"Tom, Suzette, I'd like you to meet my son, Michael, and my daughter, Kelly."

What? Now I was standing right there with Thurman Munson's children and his wife who was introducing them to us. It was all I could ever ask for— a dream come true.

Before they walked away Diana asked where we were sitting and with astonishment I told her "Table One." And she said, "We're gonna be great friends. You're sitting with us tonight."

I'm usually not speechless but I was at that moment. I asked myself how that was possible, that we weren't celebrities or family, just a couple from upstate New York. And as I took that moment in I tried my best to hide the giddiness that churned inside of me, and asked Michael and Kelly to sign their dad's book that I had since my childhood and they signed. As they walked away I said, "Wait, can I get a picture with you?" They said they had to go, and Suzette reminded me we'd be at the same table.

We took an elevator up to the reception and it looked like abut 300 tables in this huge room— nothing like I'd ever been to or seen before. I looked across that gigantic room and we started walking towards our table—the closest one to the stage. I must admit it was a pretty good feeling weaving our way to our table, knowing where we'd be seating and who we'd be with. As I approached the table I saw Michael was sitting there with an intimidating look on his face and thought that's how Thurman must have looked to the reporters. Michael's wife was there, Kelly was there and Diana's best friend Joanne from her childhood, two more friends and us. We had our salad, and we talked about Thurman and we talked about the dinner and that's when I decided to tell them about the research I'd put together about Thurman.

I felt comfortable telling them about the whole thing. They seemed very interested and wanted to know everything. Suzette told them how I grew up with Thurman and how much time I'd spent putting his statistics together and was his biggest advocate for the Hall of Fame. I told them emphatically that Thurman deserved to be in the Hall of Fame. I told them how I acquired the postcard, and they really appreciated what I had to say and what I wanted to do. Diana was mingling at other tables but Michael said my story and research was "Unbelievable."

The speeches that followed were memorable and but I couldn't stop thinking about what had happened that night. We spoke for a good while after the event had ended, and when we said our goodbyes we noticed we were the last table to leave and we were walking out with the Munson family.

As we walked out one of the men took me by the arm and said, "Go get em Tom." It wasn't just that he said it, it was the way he'd said it. There was meaning behind his tone and inflection— an affirmation for me to keep going with my cause. I wanted their respect and wanted them to understand my feelings were real and this was it. The whole day was a confirmation for me— a special day in my life— giving me even more incentive to take the lead, never look back and bring it home where it belonged.

We stayed with my sister Debbie on Long Island the next day with the whole family there to help celebrate my 50th birthday. It was a beautiful day, and they all wanted to hear my story and Suzette's story about the dinner because they knew how much it meant to me. As it turns out it was the last time we'd all be together. My brother Roy passed a few months later and my mom just one month later. But I am deeply thankful for how all of it worked out.

I don't know if all of us would have gotten together for my birthday had we not driven to New York for the Munson dinner. Perhaps we'd gather for Thanksgiving or Christmas, but not very likely. Getting that many people together was always a challenge.

In many ways, the Munson dinner was a steppingstone to our last family gathering. It's no stretch for me to believe that some greater power orchestrated the whole sequence of events, and why wouldn't it? Life had dropped a few more signs along my path and all I had to do was follow. And as I contemplate my version of what happened in such an arranged and perfect order, I am thankful and in awe of the whole thing.

Chapter 16
Larry & Brenda

*"He looked at me and said simply, "You've got this, Tom. You'll be fine."
And as he walked away he turned and said, "You're my boy."*

There are chapters in all our lives that are not always happy ones. Chapters that pull on your heart-strings, stories that make you cry or even ask what they are doing in a book like this one.

But for me, the deaths of loved ones has served to strengthen me and is part of my story, that the aftermath of picking up the pieces and sorting through tragedy has propelled me forward, knowing life has plenty of tragedy and dealing with it illustrates your character. As far as I'm concerned without these stories being told, my story wouldn't be complete, would fail in bringing my overall message in what Going the Distance means to me.

By spring of 2015, the healing process from the deaths of my brother and mom less than two years earlier was still in process. That my dad had died three years before that was just as devastating. At times I found it hard to believe that both may parents and my brother were gone.

But life did its normal give and take with us. Two grandchildren— Jack and Ava— the newest members of the next wave of Tunison's were born and the circle of life was doing its thing.

We were excited when the month of May came around, a big birthday month for us. Suzette's dad Larry, her mother Brenda, my mother, my son Jimmy, our niece, Katie, my nephew, Bobby and my niece, Sam, all celebrating birthdays bunched into three weeks of May. It was our busiest month by far and always we were together to celebrate and to give thanks.

Our celebrations usually centered around baseball and this kickoff was no different. We'd drive to West Lawn where Jimmy's college team—perennial powerhouse Misericordia Cougars—would be playing for the conference championship game. Our pre-game plan included meeting up with Larry and Brenda later— a routine we'd practiced several times in the past, but as we waited at the hotel and heard nothing from them, we became very concerned.

Larry and Brenda were always on time for the games, so we decided Suzette would stay at the hotel until they arrived, and I'd drive over to the game. It was a very tense time. We sensed something might be wrong and hoped they'd been delayed by traffic or something else, but they weren't answering our cell-phone calls, and our anxiety levels rose by the minute.

We didn't want Jimmy to be worried if we weren't at the game, but when I arrived by myself, I could tell by the look on his face he knew something wasn't right. I couldn't tell him why I was alone because I didn't know anything myself. As a matter of fact, I didn't talk to Jimmy at all during the game, tried to keep things normal by just watching the game and not showing concern for whatever might be the problem. I kept calling Suzette during the game and she still hadn't heard anything. And as the innings passed by all the way to games end, I was more focused on Larry and Brenda than on who won the game.

The second the game ended, I got the call from Suzette. She told me to get to the hotel right away, and from the tone in her voice I asked no questions. Of course I was hoping for the best and praying for them, still not knowing what had happened, but when I arrived at the hotel, Suzette was distraught. An accident on the highway... Larry killed at the scene— Brenda rushed to the hospital... fighting for her life.

We were both in shock, but functioning somehow. Suzette told me as much as she could, then started packing for the hospital and I went down to prepare the car. The team bus arrived in the parking lot, and when Jimmy got off he saw me standing there, and he knew something was terribly wrong. He came over to me and as we embraced I told him the news and that he needed to be strong.

As we went inside to the lobby, Suzette joined us and the entire team swallowed us up with hugs and tears and love. There was total silence other than the sobbing— a very emotional moment for all of us— you could feel the love and emotion surrounding us— penetrating us. But after a few minutes we told everyone we had to get to the hospital for Brenda.

Mike and Laura Vogeli volunteered to drive us to the hospital which was an hour away, Mike driving my car while Laura followed with Suzette. There was hardly a moment to process what we'd been told as we arrived at the hospital, we practically begged the hospital staff to allow us on the floor where they were performing an emergency operation on Brenda. They understood our circumstances and led us to a small, private waiting room on that floor where we waited, hoping and praying for her recovery. A short time later, the surgeon came out with that look of dejection on his face, and he didn't have to say a word. I knew she didn't make it.

It took about an hour for Suzette's siblings to arrive at the hospital where we gave them the news. Total devastation in an instant— hard to believe or even to fathom.

I understood what it was like to lose your parents, but this was different. I had time to talk and share with my parents before their deaths, but this came like a thief in the night taking all of us by surprise. That emptiness and hollowness I'd come to know returned, indescribable beyond belief. You just can't describe it properly. I lost my mom and my brother, Roy just a month apart. And when Roy called me from his hospital bed just days before his death to tell me how thrilled he was that Jack was born, I was honored he had the chance to say those words to me and I was equally honored walking Roy's daughter, Tara, down the aisle for her wedding, giving her away in his absence. And now the common factor in keeping us grounded through all that happened was gone. The rocks of our family— Larry and Brenda— taken when we needed them most. They were our everything.

As I thought about Larry, so many thoughts came to mind, thoughts that took me back to when I needed Larry most— the day I was about to give Roy's eulogy.

That morning I was pacing outside our hotel trying to collect myself. I'd never given a eulogy before and there I was, just hours away from speaking, representing our family, nervous and praying the right words would come out.

Then Larry came walking towards me dressed in his suit. He looked confident and knowing, I'm sure he sensed what I was feeling. He looked at me and said simply, "You've got this, Tom. You'll be fine." And as he walked away he turned and said, "You're my boy."

His words meant everything to me. He'd lost his only son at birth, and the connection I felt then and there was very powerful. I thought about his loss and how awful that must have felt, and that Roy's death likely brought back those deep-seated memories. Larry lost a son, and I lost a brother, and now the man I admired and respected and loved so much told me I was his boy. I swear I felt the pulse of the earth just then.

An odd calmness and peace came over me, and I was grateful for that. I'd keep that feeling inside, a warm, comforting sensation, keep it in store for future use. His words— three simple words— "You'l be fine," would stay with me, and helped me speak at Roy's eulogy. I have to be the rock. I have to be the wise one saying magical words as if written as a prescription.

So now we're back dealing with the pain of Larry and Brenda's deaths and I'm repeating those three words he said to me over and over in my mind, hoping and praying that feeling of calm and peace finds me again. And just when I needed it most, it happened.

It had been several days since their funeral when I drove to their house to cut the grass and watered the flowers. It was an eerie, empty feeling, and when I went inside I couldn't breath. I felt the air suck out of my lungs, weakening me and bringing me to my knees. And as my breathing came back slowly, I looked around at the many positive messages they had around the house, drawn to one that read, "Prayer Changes Everything." Those words were hard to ignore as I kept reading them, looking for answers and trying to make some sense of things. How ironic that Larry was a marine captain, a pilot, flying over 600 missions into enemy territory in Vietnam. He survived over 600 missions in a hostile country and dies in a car crash back home. Of course prayer couldn't bring him back, couldn't bring Brenda back. But as I kept reading those words over and over, I felt it was a sign from Larry and Brenda, to continue believing in the power of prayer, to stay the course no matter what. Both of them knew what to say and when to say it.

When Thurman died, Brenda was coaching Suzette's sister Melissa's softball team the day before they were scheduled to play in the Cinderella Softball World Series championship game. One of her players was Karen Stedman, a terrific catcher and integral part of the team, as well as a huge Thurman Munson fan— her baseball idol. Karen told Brenda she couldn't possibly play that day, that she was too upset to get on the field, distraught from by what happened. In her calming way, Brenda assured Karen that she understood, and asked her if she thought Thurman would have been happy with her decision. She went on to say that Thurman would have wanted her to play— and to play the best game of her life— that her teammates were counting on her, especially being the catcher.

Brenda's words inspired Karen. Not only did she play, her team won the championship. And while Brenda's words weren't said on her knees in prayer, to me that's what prayer can be. Words that changes everything. Inflection that changes everything. Empathy that changes everything. Prayer changes everything, I thought. It most definitely was a sign from Larry and Brenda.

And signs have always been there for me to take notice of and to understand their meaning. Signs have been easy to recognize for me, and I take them seriously and to heart. They give me hope when hope seems lost. They strengthen my faith in times of sorrow, and they inspire me to continue the fight.

I wasn't looking for a sign as I rode to the hospital with my friend, Mike Vogeli, hoping and praying that Brenda was still alive. As I gave that memory a moment and Mike drove on, the largest and most colorful sun seemed to appear in the sky out of nowhere. Neither one of us had seen a sun that big before. It seemed to be taking all the room in the sky for itself as its rays lit a nearby field. We were both awestruck and really couldn't fathom what we were seeing. It was a sign from God telling me that Larry was home, and that the sun— as beautiful as it was— would soon set like it always had. And as we learned that Brenda hadn't made it, I understood that incredible, once-in-a-lifetime experience sunset, was for both of them. It gave me the feeling not to be afraid of death... that God is there... and you don't have to look very hard to find him.

I had then privilege to sing, "Take me to the Cross" at their funeral in front of 300 people. There are times when you perform you can feel when *it's just right*— when everything comes together, and you know it. God was there with me that day making sure that it happened. With a world of emotion inside me, and hanging onto those words, *Prayer changes everything*, I believe it was my finest performance ever.

Their team had won that game on Corey Vogeli's complete game shutout victory the day of the accident, and we decided that Jimmy should stay with his team for the championship finals the next day, that Suzette would drive home to Bath with her siblings and I'd stay behind with Jimmy, giving him some family support as best we could. And they won the next day, sweeping DeSales in two games to win their conference again.

There was no Hollywood-type ending where Jimmy would come in from the bullpen to strike out their best hitter for the final out of the game or make a great fielding play to save the game. In fact, he didn't even pitch an inning. But that didn't matter so much. What really mattered was he was there with his team to share that rare moment of team victory.

Amidst all the heartbreak and sorrow, I knew that life goes on and always had lived that way. There's another day ahead, another day to seize, another game to play— not just words but concepts to live by. None of that was easy to navigate right then, but I knew that despite what we'd been through or how long it might take, we'd rise above it all together.

Chapter 17
Gordon

"This was quite a journey for me, and I held those Beatles lyrics, "When I Find Myself in Times of Trouble," close to my heart."

Just a few months later, Larry's brother, Jim, died from a heart-attack. We had already planned on spending more time with Jim and he always asked us down to his home in New Jersey. I think at that point we decided that any opportunity that came up again to visit a relative or have one visit us was one we'd take, that this was enough already. We would miss Jim dearly.

As if we didn't have enough to deal with, I suffered a major hip injury during a freak accident following Brenda's and Larry's funeral.

A neighbor had let us borrow some folding chairs, and I was preparing to break them down. I took a break after a while, sitting on one of those chairs when I noticed our dog chasing after a stray cat. As that cat ran under my chair I rose quickly to get out of the way and the chair broke sending me to the ground. I felt something tear right then and felt the pain in my hip immediately. I waited a while hoping the pain would go away, and for the most part, it did. But the pain came back in full force a bit later when I was cutting Brenda's and Larry's lawn. I went down like I'd been punched and couldn't get up. I had to call Suzette and our son, Jimmy to take me home.

I tore the labrum in my hip— the very hip that caused me to miss so much of my early childhood. It would have been easy to blame it on my Perthe's, blaming Father Time for just taking its course, or that I'd been laying floor for 25 years, playing and coaching baseball for 30 years and had overused it, or the combination of all that. But whatever it was, I was in a world of pain and I had a decision to make.

There wasn't much of a choice in the matter when the Doctor's discussed my options with me, but that option—surgery— would put me out of action for six months. Thankfully, my boss Judy Towner assured me that my job would be waiting for me when I was able to return. That was comforting news.

Of course my mind went back in time, remembering my three year struggle with Perthes, all the precautions and warning and restrictions to follow. But this was different. My parents and siblings had watched over me when I was young, caring for me and making sure I was comfortable and had whatever it was I needed. But now... now I felt the weight of the world on me. I was the adult now, the one caring for a family, the one making sure they were comfortable and given whatever it was they needed. But I was helpless—literally helpless again— and because of that and all that had happened with Brenda and Larry, I turned away from those things I loved most.

I love music but didn't want to hear a song. I liked a few shows but didn't want to watch television. I loved the Yankees and baseball but didn't want to follow how they're doing or what the standings were. I was in a deep funk, and that's when I turned to my Bible for help.

I suppose when so many horrible things happen in such a short period of time, it's easy to get down on life or even become depressed or crawl into a shell like I had done at first. I can understand how someone with a similar experience to mine could turn away from God—even abandon God— with so many trials and tribulations. I suppose that would be the easy way out.

I chose another direction when I picked up my bible and started taking notes, memorizing verses and trying to understand what was happening. It took some time to really process the bibles many messages of hope, faith and trust and before long, I started having a better outlook on things.

I hung onto my bible for dear life. I prayed differently at church, prayed differently before bedtime, prayed better and harder than I ever had in my life. I was supposed to be the rock of our family, but couldn't even pick up our grandkids. I remember praying, " God, just let me hold these children in arms. Let me walk on the beach with them again. I don't even care if I can run again or do everything I used to do, please, Lord, just let me be able to walk again."

When you're unable to walk, time can be your worst enemy or your best friend. There's time to analyze your life, your purpose in life and time to reflect on the person you are. I found myself reflecting on my life all the time.

When I thought back to my childhood, I gravitated to other boys who loved sports as much as I did. In our working-class neighborhood, we did our share of romping around and we were no angels, but none of the pranks we pulled ever landed us into any serious trouble. As I got older it was natural instinct for me to continue to gravitate towards others like me, guys who competed and played baseball, some with that dream to make it to the pros. And that was me. In the back of my mind I wanted that for myself, to be that kid to have made it to the pros, even for a while. To be able to share my story of rising up out of a hospital bed, wheelchair and crutches, to use that as motivation and inspiration for other kids with that same dream. If anything, what I'd gone through in the past was motivation enough for me. That I'd competed all the way to semi-pro baseball and contributed really good results to my teams always kept that dream alive in me. I wanted to be an influence on others, to make that difference.

I remember inviting kids to play with us if they were riding by on their bike or walking by themselves. I'd say, "You want to play with us?" because I never wanted them to not have a friend or to take part in what we were doing. It's always been easy for me to see the good in people and to reach out like that.

I'd always looked for the good in a person, always wanted to get to know them and let them know how much I care about them. I love success stories, triumph over tragedy, that sort of thing, and it doesn't take me long to figure someone out. And as I reflected on my purpose in life, Gordon Vonderlin showed up and influenced me in ways I'd never been influenced before.

He didn't play much baseball and sports wasn't his big thing. I had coached Gordon's sons in baseball, he sang in church choir with Larry and was a really nice man. But we seemed to have very little in common, so I never took the time to get to know him.

He grew up playing instruments and singing in chorus. He was just a real gentleman, a real devout Christian, so kind and funny. I had no friends growing up who played instruments or sang in the chorus. We played baseball and football and roller hockey.

I truly believe God placed Gordon in my life for a reason, how he was able to weave our paths, such different paths, onto one beautiful road. How the irony of another hip injury changed our paths just as Perthes Disease connected me to Thurman Munson.

Gordon was one of the volunteers from church along with Allan Gay, John Jones, Jim Newman and Peg Inglis who drove me to physical therapy and was where we got to know each other. And in a short time we realized how much we had in common. As I learned more about him I knew that God had a hand in all of this. His words encouraged me and humbled me at the same time. I was encouraged because of what he'd overcome and lived with, and humbled because Perthes and what I was dealing with now paled in comparison to his.

Despite reading my bible, building a budding friendship and camaraderie with Gordon and the other volunteers' drivers, there was something else I needed to speed up my recovery, and that was some tough love coming from two unlikely sources.

The Bath girls youth softball team with my niece, Skylar, had dedicated several trees in Brenda and Larry's honor and placed a beautifully engraved stone at the roots near their softball field. On opening day of softball, they held a special ceremony for Brenda and Larry, and I walked out onto the field without my crutches. When I went back inside I grabbed my crutches when a man from church—Brad Laverty— asked, "Tom, are you alright?" I said, "I'm hanging in there," and he asked again with more concern, "No, are you *alright*?"

I wasn't sure why he'd asked twice, but he pointed to his head and said, "Tom, you have to first be all-right in here." His eyes were so sincere and I understood what he was trying to tell me.

By this time I'd already gone through two physical therapists who seemed very disinterested— even apathetic to my therapy. They hadn't really taken part or gotten to know me and gave little advice or encouragement, really just going through the motions, and so was I. I hadn't really taken any advice they gave me to heart until a third physical therapist—Marc Riley— came into the picture.

My very first appointment with Marc was a turning-point moment— a tough love moment that I needed desperately. He took one look at me and said, "Tom, you're a mess and I don't know where to begin with you. But we will begin." It was at this very moment I knew this man was going to help me. But after about six weeks of visits he told me I probably should go someplace else. I said, "What do you mean?" and he said, "You keep coming in here on your crutches despite our advice. I think you should go somewhere else... unless you listen to me... If you do, then we will begin again." I said, "Thank God you said that. I needed to hear it." He gave me hope right then and there.

Three days later I walked into that office without my crutches and the whole place stopped and looked at me, including that same therapist who yelled out, "Look at this guy!"

I truly believe it was those two people that really triggered me to get over it, and later having Gordon to support me and to help me stay the course. I was in my bible and trusting in God and praying so hard that I really wasn't paying attention to myself when these three angels came into my life.

Gordon talked about the church choir all the time and pleaded with me to join. I'd been asked by others to join prior to my injury but I was always too busy or didn't really have the heart to do it and make that commitment or feel obligated. But I finally gave in and promised Gordon when I got back on my feet I would join the choir. Thank God I did because it really changed my perspective and—along with Suzette's constant care and the motivation of my grandson Nicholas being born— really helped change my way of thinking about my life because I got to know Gordon personally.

Occasionally the choir set up a drum circle with Gordon as lead drummer. They asked me to sing a song titled, *Open the Eyes of my Heart*, and it went so well we started our own *Praise Band* along with Bob Mesler, Kirk Mishrell, Jim Robinson and Carolyn Jones.

None of us had any idea how good a drummer Gordon was until then. We knew he'd been a music teacher and had to retire a few years after his heart surgery in 2004, but little did I know he played the drums like a seasoned veteran. He was so smooth with impeccable timing. A real pro.

And he was funny. We laughed at the same things. We were both big Seinfeld fans and talked about certain episodes that really got us going. We were like kids in high school at choir, trying to stifle a laugh in church but couldn't. It was just unbelievable week after week to bond like we did and to watch him play the drums and sing so well. His heart had grown weaker by the day so he was out of breath and on the brink of collapsing by the end of a session. He'd go home and tell his wife Deb how much fun he had and then texted us to tell us the same.

I'm so glad it gave him such joy. He had such a gift, such a gift.

Gordon helped take our church choir to another level participating in Christmas pageants, Children's Day in the summer and even playing in front of the church last summer—an unheard of concept before. We'd played the early church service on the steps of the church and one of the songs we'd been working on was, "Let it Be," by the Beatles, one of Gordon's favorites.

Gordon came home from the hospital for the last time and asked me to play that song at his funeral, that it was time for him to come home. When he said that to me I was shocked and I said, "What are you talking about, you're not going anywhere, you are home. You're gonna rebound like you always do." But he knew better, that his life was coming to a close and there was nothing anybody could do about it anymore. It had be hard for him knowing this, but he graced us with his presence every week. He kept coming to choir and even though he didn't have his wind to sing, he gave it everything he had. He showed me the way.

We had always wondered if, *Let It Be* was an appropriate song to sing at church. There's no lyrics about Jesus or God, but there's plenty to do with faith. Lots of people tied in the, *Mother Mary* inference with the Virgin Mary. Even Paul McCartney said that even though he wrote it was about his mother coming to him in a dream, that its lyrics were open for personal interpretation. We did play it at Gordon's funeral, but his story doesn't end like that.

Gordon was very close with Brenda and Larry— my in-laws who died in the car accident. Gordon told me a short time before he died that Brenda and Larry had planned on coming back home after the game the next day to attend a memorial service for a close friend— Dawn Chatfield— a bedrock of the church for over 50 years. Larry and Gordon were the two main tenors in the choir, so it was important that Larry came home. And like all of us when we heard the news, Gordon told me how devastated he was.

Then Gordon told me about an amazing dream he had about two years ago, one where Brenda and Larry were riding on a bus through golden skies with brilliant lights all around them, then suddenly they were sitting on the bleachers right at mid-court at my sons basketball game .

Gordon had never attended any of my sons basketball games and to my knowledge wasn't aware that Brenda and Larry attended all of them, but Gordon said he saw all this in his dream, and they were glowing, shining like the sun. He said it was absolutely incredible.

This was quite a journey for me, and I held those Beatles lyrics, *When I Find Myself In Times of Trouble,* close to my heart. New people coming into my life, new experiences that had happened for a reason, new obstacles to tackle and to grow from. And as I reflected on every bit of it, missing Jimmy's final year playing college baseball was probably the hardest pill to swallow.

We had missed hardly any of his games until now, and I wasn't concerned we'd miss any again. But when the original six week recovery period turned into six months, that turned things upside down. We had so looked forward to traveling to Puerto Rico for the teams opening tournament, but had to cancel our trip— not only devastating because we rarely missed a game, but after so many wonderful years of baseball, this would be our last hurrah. Not only was that final season not supposed to end this way, Jimmy struggled in Puerto Rico and continued to struggle as the season wore on.

I was chomping at the bit missing all his games, but when Seniors Day approached and 20 family members were set to go to the game, Suzette and her brother Matthew devised a scheme by placing me onto a bed inside his van and driving the two-and-a-half hours to Dallas, Pa., to surprise Jimmy. For the most part it was a pretty comfortable ride, and it felt good I was going to a game and not to physical therapy.

When we got to the field I spotted some players getting loose on the sidelines, then saw Jimmy running out of the dugout to warm up in the bullpen. I yelled out to him, "Hey Tunison"... he stopped in his tracks and gave me that million dollar smile of his.

Later in the game, Coach Pete Egbert called for Jimmy from the bullpen and he threw GAS, striking out their best hitter and finishing the inning. He started the next inning and in the tradition of honoring Seniors, Egbert pulled him before the inning ended and Jimmy left the mound to a standing ovation. Everyone seemed amazed at his effort. From that point forward right up to the final out of the season, Jimmy started an incredible run of pitching dominance where he was untouchable.

We returned home, and I'd watch the rest of their games that year on the computer. Whenever Jimmy entered the game I would pray for him, his mates and the other teams players safety against injury, then root like heck for him.

There seemed to be so many times Coach Egbert brought him into the game with the bases loaded and the game on the line, and every time he'd pitch out of a jam, stranding the runners in place. Jimmy told me later that whenever he entered the game he would picture Suzette and me standing by the dugout, and that it brought him peace to get through his situation.

He carried his great run right into the postseason, earning the save in the semi-final conference championship game at West Lawn Pa. – the very field they played on the year before— the field when I first learned about the accident.

They won the championship the next day, Jimmy primed and ready in the bullpen to come in for the final out. But his teammate nailed it down and Misericordia celebrated a sixth consecutive championship.

Chapter 18
Batavia Downs

"I felt strongly that I needed to be in Batavia that day— there was no doubting that— and how I needed to trust that inner voice and follow it, wondering what would have happened if I chose to stay home that day."

I'd known for a while a baseball card show had been scheduled about an hour north of us at Batavia Downs, and that Ron Guidry was one of the players who'd be signing autographs and talking baseball. Guidry was another one of my heroes and the chance to meet him in such close proximity was tempting to say the least.

But I'd been working a lot as of late and had looked forward to an easy day off, spending time at home with my wife, just relaxing and enjoying some peace and quiet. We had a very busy life, and days off to rewind and recoup was needed for both of us, especially feeling as worn out as I did from a tough week at work.

I felt depleted of energy and zapped of strength and realized there was a good chance I'd bypass the card show, that staying home was what was needed more. And being that it had been rainy and cold for a few days, with the mother of all storms that very day, hunkering down inside a warm house with my wife had me leaning towards staying home and not driving through a monsoon.

I really battled with myself what to do that day. Future chances to meet Ron Guidry crossed my mind several times— especially since he'd be right up the road in my neck of the woods. Guidry was a pitcher— just like I was— and he'd thrown so many games to Thurman during his career. I knew what Thurman meant to him, knew what he'd meant to all the pitchers, and having the chance to discuss that and other things baseball with him one-on-one was on my mind as I contemplated my decision.

Batavia Downs was normally just an hour away, but that pelting, wind-driven rain was relentless, likely adding at least another 30 minutes to the drive. Huge puddles formed on the yard, creating what looked to be a series of tiny Lakes, and the streets ran fast and hard with rain water— too fast for any drain to keep up with. Considering the amount of rain that had fallen so quickly, I was certain the nearby Cohocton River would jump its banks and cause major delays on the roads. To risk even driving under such conditions was questionable, and had to be considered in my decision.

The weather and feeling so lethargic was making for what seemed to be an easy and logical decision. But is wasn't that easy. The fact that I'd written and published an article with Chris Hahn (Thurman Munson's Decade of Unmatched Excellence) that went deep inside Thurman's numbers just a few months earlier weighed on my mind as well. This wasn't just any article. Together we felt as if our research into Thurman's career was likely the most comprehensive compilation that had been done to date. In fact, neither of us had seen or read anything quite like it before on any player. We'd spent countless hours of research into Thurman's statistics, comparing and contrasting him to Hall of Fame catchers, blended with traditional baseball statistics and new ones that had made serious inroads into the game. It was these new statistics that excited us as we burned the midnight oil looking to capture results to what we hoped would be highly favorable ones for Thurman's case.

When you're researching the way we did, there's a certain amount of tension, anxiety and excitement, with no results or standings available until the whole thing was complete. Logging numbers of such a high number of players— 30 or more— was a time consuming task. But we felt confident that what we'd uncover with the new metrics would make a difference in the way sportswriters and fans viewed Thurman Munson's career. We'd grown tired of reading internet comments of how short Thurman's career was, or how he didn't hit for power, how he'd slowed down at the end. We'd debated on-line with his detractors and didn't understand why people were saying what they were about him. It bothered me and bothered me a lot. And despite the fact that neither of us were sportswriters or known names in the baseball world, we weren't about to let that deter us. We felt it was time to do something about it.

As I thought about our Munson research, a 22 page labor of love we titled, Thurman Munson's Decade of Unmatched Excellence, I thought about my Baseball Academy plan. I could hardly believe seven years had passed since that plan had been developed and set into motion— my first foray into looking inside the numbers of dozens of overlooked players for the Hall of Fame. And it seemed like something always was happening that prevented me from taking it one step further— family, work, other responsibilities—and for seven long years, it lay dormant. But it had always been in the back of my mind— always.

So much had happened during those seven years— life-changing events that so rocked my world I felt there was no choice but to put my dream of building my Baseball Academy on hold. And during those few times when it seemed to be the right time to proceed, when life seemed to give me a sliver of hope to go on, something else came along, something that took precious time away from going the distance with it.

I wasn't about to let any delays get me down or to start feeling sorry for myself. I'd learned that way of thinking was not only a useless waste of time and energy but wasn't in my makeup. I'd shaped my life around positivity and surrounding myself and my family with positive people, doing my best to live my life with that in mind. And on those infrequent times when being overly tired brought me down a notch, I'd pull myself in, reminding myself that by the grace of God, and at some point in my life, the Baseball Academy concept would become a reality, and that by putting my faith in my faith that time would come. I'd need to exercise some major patience in however long it might take.

But a greater urge had taken root in me. Thurman Munson for the Hall of Fame seemed more important now. We'd done the research and written our paper, but with no clearcut strategy going forward, opportunities like meeting Run Guidry had potential. Guidry had connections. He loved Thurman Munson. And while I was uncertain what he could or would do for us, I was just as certain he'd support our effort. My Baseball Academy would reward others. The time for Thurman was now... I'd go to Batavia to meet Ron Guidry.

I drove for about five miles and tried fending off fatigue but nothing seemed to be working. I thought an extra cup of coffee and a cold shower would do the job but it didn't seem to help much. I toyed with the idea of turning back, to go back home and spend the day with my wife, but I kept on driving.

I heard that guiding voice just then—almost as if on cue. It prompted me to stay the course, not to turn around but to keep driving to Batavia Downs. That was all the convincing I needed. I blurted out, "Do it Tom!"

I was feeling better now. And with more energy, ambition and curiosity, I took the remaining time before arriving at the show to think things over. I felt so very right about the decision to attend the show and hoped I'd get some time to spend with Ron Guidry, to give him a copy of our Munson research and to get his autograph on my copy. I thought also that perhaps other baseball celebrities would be in attendance, that maybe I'd get lucky and meet someone else who could help our Munson cause. I'd mingle around and hope for the best.

My wife's brother Matthew and nephew Caleb had driven separately so I knew I'd meet up with them at some point during the day. I paid my way in, got my ticket to get Ron's autograph and walked over to the line leading to his table. It didn't take too long to get to him. I'd been rehearsing what I wanted to say and was excited to meet him. I had no idea if he was gruff or talkative or standoffish. When I shook his hand and introduced myself, I felt totally comfortable. He was low-key and struck me as an easy guy to carry on a conversation with. I spoke for a few minutes about our research then handed him a copy and stated confidently that Thurman should be in The Hall of Fame.

My goal was getting signatures from every ex-Yankee players, coaches, managers, scouts and trainers from those championship seasons of 1977 and 1978 onto my copy of our research paper. I knew it was an ambitious goal and would take a lot of time, but I'd been off to a good start, landing signatures of Roy White and Bucky Dent a few months earlier at another show. But that show had a whole different feel to it. Long lines and short conversations was the norm. I gave copies of our research to both players, but there was no time for chit-chat. Like cattle the line just kept moving. I did what I could with the time I had to explain our research to both men, but I had no way of knowing what they'd do with it. I hoped they'd share it with others, that perhaps it would land on the lap of someone who could help. Perhaps that way of thinking was a long-shot, but it was something. They say it's a small world and for good reason sometimes. Believing strongly that something could happen, that something could come of it, I said a prayer over their copies and kept on moving.

And here I was, standing with Ron Guidry, handing him a copy and not being whisked away by some line attendant at a packed show. There was time to talk here. To talk about our research and to let him know how I felt about Thurman Munson. To let him know what we were doing to get Thurman into the Hall of Fame. And after only a minute or two I stated more confidently a second time that Thurman should be in The Hall of Fame.

He nodded and immediately began talking about what the experience was like pitching to Thurman. "If I threw a pitch he didn't like, he'd come out and chew me out and I'd say, easy Thurman. I put it right there where you wanted it." Guidry then took his hand and pulled his fingers apart a fraction of an inch and said, "Thurman would say, I want it right there," and walked back to the plate.

The area he'd pointed out was no wider than a postage stamp. An incredibly precise target only a perfectionist would expect from his pitcher. I thought about my days as a pitcher and knew how difficult such an expectation would be. Sure, I wasn't a pro like Ron Guidry, but I took pride in my control and hitting the target where my catcher wanted it. It gave me yet another reason to admire Thurman Munson, that such a presumption placed on his pitcher was final with no room for debate.

Guidry said, "That guy was tough. I never, ever met anybody who wanted to win more than Thurman Munson. I'd tell him we couldn't win every game. We just can't." And he'd say, "Yes, Ron. We can win every game."

Those words would stay with me from then on. The cliche, "You can't win them all," had new meaning for me. Of course I'd heard it said after a tough loss or after a game we should have won. I'd probably said it myself a few times over the years. It was one of those sayings that probably was said by anybody who'd ever played team sports. Professional baseball seasons are 162 games long—every team loses at least 60 games every year— but Thurman Munson's mindset was that of not just a winner but that of a champion— a top of the heap champion. A champion who held firm to that notion that you can win them all. It was no wonder, I thought, that he was Yankee Captain, and I loved him even more than before.

I got Ron Guidry's autograph on my copy of the article, right alongside Roy White's and Bucky Dent's. I'd cherish that signature with the respect it deserved, and felt blessed to have it. I wouldn't sell it or auction it off— ever. Ron Guidry was part of my Yankees, a teammate and battery-mate of my hero, Thurman Munson. This wasn't just another signature. It was memories. It was history. It was a connection. A connection hard to describe.

After some time, Ron got up to catch his plane and as he left the room I'd noticed he'd left behind the two copies of the article I'd given him. That's when some newspaper guy ran after him waving the copies in the air. Luckily, he made it in time. He handed the copies to Guidry, and he was gone.

I looked across the room and saw my nephew and wife's brother and proudly showed them the autograph Ron had signed for me. They took a look then told me they'd just met Dwier Brown. "Dwier Brown? From Field of Dreams?" I asked. "The very same," they said.

I went over to his table where he was just standing there alone. I introduced myself and let him know how much I appreciated his efforts in the movie, that it was my favorite baseball movie of all time. I told him how much I loved the scene when he's having a catch with his dad, what a beautiful and touching moment it was— especially knowing he'd lost his own dad during the filming of the movie.

It made me think back to the tragedies I'd faced with my family, the circumstances and timing almost too hard to fathom— ones that tested your faith and made you ask questions about life— especially the loss of my wife's parents who'd been driving to a baseball game to see their grandchild play ball, an ordinary day we'd all looked forward to gone so horribly wrong. And as that thought came and left, it struck me right then that I had formed some sort of bond with Dwier Brown— a connection formed from what life gives us and what life takes away. We'd met only a few minutes earlier, yet that feeling was strong. I looked in his eyes and said again, "What a beautiful and touching moment it really was." That's when he asked reverently, "Can I give you a hug?"

I opened my arms, and we hugged like two guys who'd known each other their whole lives. A good, hearty hug that you don't forget. And as we hugged for just those few scant seconds, I couldn't help thinking back to the day several years earlier when I'd met Diana Munson for the first time at the New York fundraiser, those words Dwier Brown had just said to me, the exact ones I'd said to Diana, "Can I give you a hug?" And that hug from her— that tight, authentic, meaningful hug— identical as the one just shared with Dwier. I could hardly believe how the day was playing out.

Our conversation turned to Thurman Munson and the effort to get him into Cooperstown, and as I explained the article Chris and I had written, my nephew Caleb walked by and Dwier yelled out his name. That may have been insignificant to Dwier, but not for me. I was deeply impressed that he'd remembered Caleb's name from earlier in the day— that he wasn't just another patron who'd purchased his book. It seemed obvious to me how important it was for Dwier to remember his name— a quality I totally respect and admire. I bought a copy of his book right then.

We had our picture taken together— one he didn't charge for. Then I asked him if he'd like a copy of the article we'd written, that it would be my pleasure to give him one. After talking more about Thurman and the articles contents, he seemed very interested and said he'd like one.

He took the book I'd purchased and wrote on the back, "Tom and Suzette... if you build it... Thurman will come" and signed it, "Dwier Brown, John Kinsella, Field of Dreams." He paused then said, "Tom. It's gonna happen. It's gonna happen. Go the distance, Tom." The way he said those words ignited the fire inside me. Encouraging words I'd heard before, but this... this was different. This was so genuine, so sincere and so emotional and it struck a chord in me that no matter what the obstacle, no matter what trial I may face, no matter how many people would tell me I was wasting my time and no matter how tired I may feel, I would stay the course. I'd build my Academy— build it for others like Ray Kinsella built his Field of Dreams. I'd push and fight for Thurman. I'd go the distance.

With adrenaline flowing through my veins, I sprinted out to my truck like a track star to get Dwier's copy. I sprinted back inside, handed Dwier a copy and asked him if he'd sign my copy. He took his pen and wrote on the back, "Go The Distance."

The ride home that night was euphoric. Drowsiness and lack of spark had been replaced by a renewed sense of purpose and an indescribable energy. I began processing the whole, amazing, wonderful day— filled with important connections I didn't see coming— and so many memories of my journey. I thought about the words Thurman had said to Ron Guidry, that, "Yes, we can win them all," and really took it to heart. And I wondered if Ron Guidry bought into it—especially the year he went 25-3— almost winning them all. I played back my hug with Dwier Brown, how it so reminded me so of Diana Munson, and felt so alive because of it. And as my mind replayed the two special messages Dwier Brown had written, I wondered if he'd written these very messages before to others— his catch phrase if you will.

But that didn't matter at all. Not one bit. I took his messages as if I'd been his only customer. That his special messages were highly significant and words I needed to follow. I felt strongly that I needed to be in Batavia that day— there was no doubting that— and how I needed to trust that inner voice and follow it, wondering what would have happened if I chose to stay home that day.

Nothing.

I saw that day for what it was, and gave thanks to the almighty for aligning things in such perfect order. Doors were opening. People I needed to meet— destined to meet— were right there now. I'd read the signs life had provided and followed them. The path— my path— was clearer now.

Chapter 19
A Committee Is Formed: Binghamton I

"It felt like the first pitch of a ball game to me. Butterflies and nerves all over the place. I'd never been in front of a camera before, didn't know what to expect."

The episode at Batavia Downs brought a new sense of determination and drive within me. I leaned on the events of that day to help fuel the fire that raged inside me, to keep the momentum alive to whatever was happening.

I'd had some time to really think about the significance of that day and needed to keep that feeling inside and to keep the momentum growing. I wasn't sure what that exactly meant or what I was supposed to do or was going to do next, but I was darn sure that all that had happened in Batavia Downs was no accident, and that I was *involved* now more than ever as some sort of instrument involving Thurman Munson, and I mean that sincerely.

It was quite exciting— and humbling— believing so strongly that I needed to stay faithful and true to whatever was happening now. I had to keep believing that my responsibility in "Going The Distance" had reached a new level and that I needed to continue following the signs life had provided. I know that may sound crazy to some people, and that's understandable.

There are signs everywhere that most of us understand. Stop Signs, Speed Signs, traffic signals, sales signs, all of it. And there are other signs we don't understand. Some of it may be due to language, not knowing translation of words. The signs are there, we just haven't learned *the language to* understand and react accordingly.

Baseball has it's own language. A third base coach touches his cap and does it again, flashing a sign to the batter that only he and his teammates understand. The other team can only guess what it means, but they can't follow that sign or make sense of it. They don't recognize any of the signs and instead resort to a guessing game of sorts trying to figure out what they may mean.

The same can be said about Life's signs. They are there and there in abundance— we need only to recognize them for what they are— and by looking closely enough, begin understanding them. That's how I felt about the Chinese Fortune Cookie, The Thurman Munson Postcards and Batavia Downs. One by one they aligned themselves into some sort of order for me to follow and I had bought into. *Too many coincidences already,* and more to come.

I studied our research paper until I had the whole thing memorized, entirely baffled and angered as to why Thurman hadn't been inducted into the Hall of Fame, still thinking about such paltry support had come his way through all those years he remained on the ballot. Just thinking about that was enough to keep me focused. And as a reminder, I started reading the fortune cookie message I'd kept with me since 2010, *Beware The Fury of a Patient Man,* just to keep the juices flowing.

I couldn't sleep. I tossed and turned. I started waking up in the middle of the night and found myself obsessing over the data, studying even more statistics, not only on Thurman, but other catcher's and especially Hall of Fame catchers. I found new data that supported my beliefs and continued finding data— some of it obscure— but all of it meaningful— all of it supporting and emphasizing what I had discovered about Thurman, that he hands down belonged in The Hall of Fame. Then one morning I took a short break from researching and that's when it hit me.

Sure, I'd done the research and kept adding on, but what good would it do unless all of it fell into the right hands? I'd given copies to a few of Munson's teammates, to Dwier Brown and a few baseball friends— hoping they in turn would get it to people in the know—people who could make a difference, but that wasn't going to be enough. I wanted badly to get it out to the masses, but had no connections to those baseball writers I'd targeted.

In the summer of 2017, my research partner Chris Hahn told me about a website he'd discovered that he'd been posting on. I didn't need to be told twice about it, and when I first opened The *Thurman Munson Fan Club* page I thought I'd struck gold. A website— fully dedicated to Thurman Munson came right up, and there were hundreds of followers.

I couldn't believe what I was reading. Dozens of comments about Thurman, stories and memories, photos and observations, replies and rebuttals. I was flabbergasted. I had felt so alone before, and now... now I'd discovered an entire community of Thurman Munson fans. I turned to that site every day simply drawn to it like I would have to a long lost friend or loved one, leaning on every word from every person because they loved Thurman like I did.

It took about two weeks for me to finally join and post something, and right away got a response from Adrienne Statfeld, the site coordinator. There was really something special about Adrienne. She posted something new every day about Thurman and it was always interesting, be it a photo, a fact or a question, she was on it. I knew the site would flourish under her capable hands.

As comments and statistics I'd posted began drawing an interest from others, some were being shared. I finally felt some sense of gratification knowing the research I'd done with Chris Hahn was getting some play, and because of that it stood a better chance of being seen by those in the know. With that hope in mind I kept reading and posting and responding to Thurman naysayers on line, feeling involved and relevant to the cause more than I ever had before. But something more needed to be done for Thurman and I knew it. The past year had been the best by far at making inroads and when the Thurman Munson Facebook page was established in 2018 it gave us another forum to sound off on, one to build participation and followers who could better understand my position and what I'd been sharing through my on-going research. On top of that, my grandson Brayton was born and I was feeling blessed beyond measure! By early 2019, things really started to heat up.

February marked the 39th anniversary of the AHRC New York City Foundation's annual fundraiser/awards dinner, the very one we'd attended in 2013 when we first met Diana Munson and her family. Suzette and I had been invited by New York lawyer and fellow Munson advocate Larry Schnapf, as well as Munson website guru Adrienne Statfeld, both who we'd met on-line. Larry had collaborated with Chris Hahn regarding starting a Hall of Fame petition for Thurman, seeking his permission to use the statistics we'd assembled. That's when Chris had Larry contact me for my approval, which I heartily agreed to.

It was another one of those moments when I knew something special was building. By now I'd posted many of our stats on line about Thurman and had received hundreds of comments and likes. And while there was quite an outpouring of support that kept the juices flowing, the cream was rising to the top. Adding Larry to the likes of Adrienne Statfeld gave us a solid start to what was needed going forward. And when Larry and I bantered around the idea of forming a Thurman Munson Hall of Fame Committee, we decided what better place could there be to finalize our roles and even make an announcement than at the AHRC Awards dinner.

To hear Yankee broadcaster Michael Kay announce to the crowd that our *Thurman Munson Hall of Fame Committee* had been formed was surreal, and that I was part of it was almost *unreal*. That something like this had been a dream of mine since I was a kid just put me into the stratosphere. I really had a hard time believing it. As things settled down and a few people recognized it was us, I couldn't help but notice Diana's smile as she looked our way. *This was big time now*, I thought, and results would be expected from a committee. We may have been smiling and celebrating a bit on the outside, but I knew the work was just beginning.

By now, thousands of Munson fans had joined our fan page, we posted a petition seeking signatures and support for Thurman and announced ourselves and our purposes to those followers. Excitement, support and well-wishes was growing exponentially. Just three weeks later Schnapf reached out to sportswriter Tim Botos of the *Canton Repository* and he wrote an article entitled, *Support Growing to get Thurman Munson in Baseball Hall of Fame.*

It was a strategic move by Schnapf to start the ball rolling where Thurman lived most of his life, the article explaining our cause and linking to 10 key stats I'd uncovered about Thurman that even *most baseball* people wouldn't have known.

That article brought some attention from others with the same interests and passion for Thurman— others wanting to join our committee— starting with New York State Baseball Hall of Fame executive director Rene LeRoux.

Schnapf had a few ongoing conversations with LeRoux by then, and was impressed with him. Larry suggested to me, Suzette and Adrienne that we bring Rene aboard as the Chair of our committee. At the time I was fairly comfortable with the setup we'd established with Schnapf running the show, but could see the potential in just the outreach and contacts I assumed LeRoux had. No sooner had we agreed to putting Rene in charge when Larry gave me the phone number of another person interested by the name of Gary Kaschak.

As head writer for the *Dummy Hoy Hall of Fame Committee*, Gary had made the right connections in the past, and knew some of voters, their emails and contact info. And he'd sent us the proposals he'd written on Hoy— brilliantly researched— appealing to the eye and more than convincing. We knew he could help us and that he wanted to.

It was during our first conversation and before I'd read his Hoy proposals that I knew he should be part of our committee. We hit it off right away, almost as if we'd known each other our whole lives, kindred spirits if you will. We talked about Munson, how Gary found out about us and what he could contribute with his research, writing and connections. I didn't hesitate or contact our other committee members for their approval. I invited him into our committee on the spot.

Our committee of four had grown to six, then dropped to five when Suzette bowed out, and I knew our roles weren't yet clear and needed too be defined. As a leader, Rene understood this as well and immediately established weekly conference calls with our first one introducing us to a strategy he was confident in, utilizing the skill sets each of us brought to the table.

Rene assigned Larry to media connections; Adrienne managing the webs sites; Gary conducting interviews and writing proposals to the voters and I'd continue researching statistics, formulating charts and adding as much as I could find to help Munson's cause. Rene would piece it all together via his many contacts and a seasoned approach to the politics at hand.

Within one week, Kaschak set up a radio interview and TV interview at WBNG in Binghamton, New York. As a native to Binghamton, Kaschak saw Thurman play in person at old Johnson Field in 1968— something I marveled at—and had his Binghamton connections. And since I was only 90 minutes away and Gary knew the turf, it was decided that the two of us would represent the committee on the interview.

Kaschak had reached out also to Jim Maggiore, editor for the Binghamton Rumble Ponies booster club newsletter — the team a minor league affiliate of the NY Mets, and to Steve Popolski, marketing director of the Rumble Ponies. Maggiore promised to write a segment about our cause in an upcoming issue, and Popolski invited us to NYS&G Stadium, for both a tour of the stadium and the unveiling of a mural featuring Binghamton's stars of the past— including Thurman Munson—ironically happening that very same day. I thought about that probability as I started my 90 minute drive to Binghamton, but was focusing on what I wanted to say at the interview.

We pulled into the parking lot of the TV station at exactly the same time. That Gary had driven in from New Jersey that morning from another direction with its own set of traffic issues and to pull in together was uncanny. It wasn't an amazing coincidence, but others would soon follow and continue to bless us. We greeted each other in the parking lot then put on our suit jackets and went inside. We had both dressed in suit and tie— representing Thurman with our Sunday best. We discussed out strategy and went inside.

It felt like the first pitch of a ball game to me. Butterflies and nerves all over the place. I'd never been in front of a camera before, didn't know what to expect. And while I'd rehearsed and memorized what I wanted to say, I was representing Thurman Munson— *Thurman Munson*, me, Tom Tunison... representing Thurman Munson.

It was at this point my mind went back in time for a few seconds. *The wheelchair... the crutches... Rizzuto on Thurman... The World Series victories... the MVP... Captain... Family man... The plane crash... Dwier Brown... The committee... Diana... Mike... Kelly... All of it...*

And now I felt more than just the responsibility in the moment. I was grateful. I was humbled. I was honored. I was in awe of how the universe had led me here today. No longer did I feel nervous, but felt a soothing ease— a comforting feeling like a warm blanket— covering me and protecting me.

When we walked into the studio we were shown the stage and above it we could see our names across the marquee. Host Kara Conrad walked out, introduced herself to me and asked Gary how he was. He'd been a guest on her show a year earlier, a book he'd written with Binghamton connections the topic of the day. And as she positioned us in our seats and had us look at the cameras and teleprompter, we were rolling.

My nervousness was replaced by confidence as Kara asked questions about Thurman. She bounced questions back and forth between us, some about his time playing in Binghamton and others about our committee and why we were there. It seemed like the whole production took a few minutes, but I felt we nailed it.

We'd gone on air a bit earlier than scheduled, so when we left the studio we decided to call the Rumble Ponies to see if we could come early for our tour of their stadium. We changed out of our dress cloths and when Gary called the stadium and started talking to Steve Popolski, he put his phone speaker on and asked Steve to repeat what he'd just said.

"As you both know we're taping segments for our mural today, people from our booster's club to talk about each player on the mural. Whatever is said about a particular player will be placed on a loop, right next to the mural so fans can listen to what was said. It's a big deal." Steve paused then said, "We had someone representing every player on the mural, but at the last minute the person chosen to speak about Thurman bowed out and today is the only day we have for taping."

We looked at each other with a sense of what was coming next, and when Steve said, "I know it's last minute and you'll have little time to prepare, but we were hoping you guys could handle that.... you know... speak about Thurman."

I think both of us shook our heads in disbelief as we told Steve we'd be honored. We headed for the ballpark, taking that 15 minutes to prepare what we might say, then headed into the stadium where Steve met us at the front gate.

The mural was a blending of Binghamton's top players past and present, painted along a 15' section of wall just inside the main entrance, adjacent to the ticket office. We squatted close to the Thurman Munson painting, posing for photos and admiring its work. We toured the stadium, went inside the press box, the dugouts and into the the locker room to meet up with the rest of the folks from the boosters club who'd been chosen for the taping.

We introduced ourselves to those around us, some who were reading from their notes, practicing their lines, while others milled around the room. As Gary shook the hand of an elderly gentleman, he perked up as if he'd just met a celebrity. After a few minutes Gary said, "Tom, I want you to meet John Fox, the best sports writer this town ever had. He's one of my heroes."

The two of them talked about Binghamton sports from when Gary lived there back in the 70's, and as they reminisced about the good old days, I kept thinking to myself how the day kept playing out.

We followed Steve and the others down a long set of stairs leading to what looked to be a dungeon. It was dark and cold, poorly lit and a bit tricky to navigate. In the distance I noticed a portion of the room had been cordoned off, a dark backdrop, some cameras set on pedestals next to a crew of three or four people. They brought us in, gave us a few pointers and positioned the first person to begin taping.

They went through the entire list of people before getting to us. We couldn't help but notice each of them had read their lines from pages they'd typed or hand-written, and when our turn finally came, we stood next to each other ready to wing it.

Gary went first, sharing a few memories he had watching Thurman play for the Triplets back in 1968. I was really drawn to what he had to say, those few first hand accounts of Thurman's hustle and desire still fresh on his mind. He segued to me like we'd rehearsed it, and when I finished talking about as many of Thurman's accomplishments there'd been time for, the entire gallery of people stood and clapped for us. One take and it was done.

We went to lunch with Jim Maggiore where he interviewed us for the Rumble Ponies newsletter, then to downtown Binghamton where a sports memorabilia store was selling old Triplets paraphernalia, hoping to find something related to Thurman. While that search came up short and we walked the downtown streets of Binghamton, we headed to dinner at a local Italian restaurant.

We sat at the bar and watched our TV segment from earlier in the day on our cell phones several times. I would not have thought in a million years we'd look and appear as polished as we were for that TV interview, and then to receive a standing ovation from our Munson taping after that was incredible. We sat there together for a couple of hours, as if we'd known each other for years— kindred spirits fo sure. We reviewed what turned out to be the most perfect day, and while we still found it hard to believe the many *coincidences* that had occurred and how everything fell into place like it had, we really weren't surprised at all.

We shared such similar beliefs in all of it, how life's paths align in such ways. It was good to have a new friend with the same ideals and beliefs that I had, someone who'd shared some of his experiences and could sense— could know— that there was something bigger at work here. When we paid our bill and walked out to the parking lot of the restaurant, we hugged like brothers and promised to stay in touch.

The ride home was similar to the ride home after meeting Dwier Brown at Batavia Downs. I kept the radio off and just let my mind go free at the wonder of it all. And as I thought about my role in going the distance for

Thurman, the experiences I had that day in front of the camera and in front of a crowd gave me a foundation to work with and to run with. I wasn't afraid or apprehensive to appear on TV or in front of a camera anymore. I gained confidence and felt comfortable in such a setting and knew— if given the chance—I could be a voice for Thurman.

Chapter 20
The Munson Ball

"There was a slight pause in our conversation when Gary said, "Yes, Tom. I'm giving you the ball. And I'm giving the patch to Adrienne."

Adrienne Statfeld posted our TV interview the next day on the Munson Fan Page and the response was enormous. To get exposure on TV was big in a sense that it reached a lot of people outside of our Fan Page, opening up more possibilities that someone in the inner-loop of Hall of Fame voters could have tuned in or had someone who had watched it share it with them.

Soon enough Kaschak was interviewed by Roger Neel of WNBF radio, Binghamton, then John Jennings from KKLN Minnesota had us both on the air. The national attention we'd received from the article written in Canton to Binghamton to Minnesota gave us solid traction as we pressed on for more.

It felt great getting exposure from around the country, to get hundreds of people adding their signatures to our petition, but all of us on the committee new it wasn't going to be enough to get Thurman inducted. And while more and more people joined the Fan Club and shared their feelings about Thurman, our target audience wouldn't be so easy to crack or to even get in contact with.

Kaschak had been through it before on a prior committee he'd served on and shared his frustrations from that experience starting with the 11 member baseball Historical Overview Committee, sort of a like a scouting party that assembled a list of potential Hall of Famers for the Veteran's Committee's final vote. They'd been difficult to contact, its mostly seasoned baseball writers ignoring or not seeing proposals Gary had emailed to them personally and to the Hall of Fame.

And while Gary broke through and had conversations with two of the 11, he'd been told that written proposals— no matter how well researched or convincing— were likely to have hit the slush pile, due in part to the deluge of proposals written by other groups supporting other players and the fact that these were baseball historians who knew the turf. They didn't need any help.

But that was the point, really. Surface numbers of every player in baseball history had been painstakingly researched and posted on Baseball Reference, these new measures of statistics *enhancing* Thurman's case for the Hall of Fame. I'd taken those numbers and reached as far inside of them as I could go, undeterred, determined and confident that the soapbox I'd been preaching on for years was more like a ladder now, far-reaching with an audience growing exponentially by the day.

But we all knew we'd need more than a ladder to climb the mountain needed to reach the voters, and despite the obstacle course we'd need to navigate that rugged terrain, Rene kept us on course. He seemed to know everyone in baseball and constantly reached out to many of them, his persuasive nature seeking both support and counsel. Adrienne masterfully added solid content every single day to the Fan Sites (and continues doing so), Larry made inroads with his media contacts, I continued digging up more stats and Gary was put on the trail of Thurman's past.

Each role had a purpose designed to bring it all together— proposals combining statistics, quotes made about Thurman from people both in and out of baseball and first-hand stories from people who knew Thurman before going pro. That assignment was given to Gary.

When I first heard about Gary reaching out to Thurman's friends I was pleased in a number of ways. These people knew Thurman Munson in his youth. The fact that Gary got to talk to them personally, well, I was really happy for him. I'm happy for people when they get to do meaningful things. We spoke every day about who he'd reached and what they had to say about Thurman. It was a new layer for me as Gary pulled me inside, a layer that opened a door that led to a window of Thurman's youth, of

Canton's past. And as Gary shared those snapshots, those point-of-views from so many others, my admiration of Thurman Munson reached an all-time high.

When I read a quote from Thurman's Kent State college coach "Moose" Paskert, I wasn't surprised at all. That Paskert said, "He reincarnated the pickoff play, and he educated the American baseball fan in the dyed-in-the-wool art of hitting behind the runner. He was the greatest at hitting behind the runner of any baseball player I have ever seen."

Childhood friend Joe Gilhausen had this to say, "He was such a great natural athlete. I saw it first hand when we played Pony ball together. We went 54-0, and he was our star player. But you know what I remember most about Thurman? He was a team-first guy who wanted all of us to share in victories. I was a sophomore running back on our high school team when Thurman was a senior. He was our starting back and rarely came out of the game. On those rare occasions when they took him out for a breather, he would yell to our quarterback, "Give Joe the ball." And he did that every single time I went in for him. It was important for him that I got involved." Gilhausen paused then said, "You know what kind of guy Thurman Munson was? Unselfish, that's what he was. He loved his teammates, and he loved his team. I'll never forget him for that. One thing that really separated him from other great players was he truly believed no pitcher could get him out, and if they did, it was an accident— especially on rare occasions when he'd strike out. That kind of mindset made him a standout."

Perhaps the story told by long time local high school baseball coach Doug Miller had the most significance for me. It was during one of Munson's many days when he and some friends were whacking the ball around for fun, when he was noticed by Ralph Miller—Doug's father—coach of the local Seran Agency team. That Ohio Inter- city League was a tough league, full of ex- minor leaguers and semi-pros. Serious players that wanted to win. And as Miller just by chance caught a glimpse of Munson hitting the stuffing out of the ball, he pulled his car over for a better look. Doug, bat boy for the team, remembers that day well. Dad asked, "Who is that?" "Thurman Munson," I said. "Let's go ask him to play for us. And we did." Aside from any of the numerous baseball, football or basketball stories Gary had uncovered about Thurman, it was the off-field ones— more like parables, really —that had my attention most.

I'd always believed and tried leading my life with humility, dignity and never bragging of accomplishments or what I may have done to have helped a fellow human being through difficult times. I suppose some of that is due in part to those who'd helped me when I needed it most, selfless acts of sacrifice and simply *doing the right thing* Whatever the reason, that's inside of me and always has been. It's who I am. And it's an attribute I admire most in others.

I'd learned some time ago about Thurman's silent contributions to needy causes, his private visits to sick kids in the hospital, under-the-radar visits void of press or media coverage of any kind. So when I read Gary's story of Ron Lemmo, well, that's when my Thurman Munson barometer hit a new level.

"I played for Canton-McKinley (high school) back then, and Thurman played for Canton-Lehman," recalled Ron Lemmo. "Thurman was in his senior year and I was just a skinny sophomore second baseman. I remember having two solid hits in the game, but Thurman hit a homer, the only run in that game. We formed lines and shook hands after the game, and Thurman said to me, "Way to hit the ball, little man."

"I wish I could turn on a curveball the way you can," Lemmo recalls saying to Munson. "Without hesitation, Thurman Munson says to me, "Meet me down at Cook Park tomorrow. I'll throw you some curves. Show you how it's done." Lemmo paused and said, "Thurman Munson said that to me *as if he knew* I was going to ask him for help. And I'm glad that he did."

Lemmo credits Munson, in part, helping him become an All-Ohio second basemen two years later. "He spent some quality time with me, offering tips on how to hit and time the curve. Me... an opponent... *who does that?* And you know what? We were friends from that point on."

And Steve Fettman, a Canton native and chair of the *Thurman Munson Catcher's Award*, recalled the day in 1978 right after the World Series, saying, "A few of us were riding our bikes— sixth and seventh graders— trying to get the courage up to knock on his door, to ask for his autograph. He saw us out there, dressed in his bath robe and he let us in. He gave us his autograph. I still have that autograph today."

It was just a few weeks later when Gary reached out to tell me that Doug Miller had sent him three Thurman Munson treasures he'd kept *for over 50 years*. Miller had told him he couldn't think of a better person to have them, that the efforts being made to get Thurman into Cooperstown need not go unrewarded.

Of course I was thrilled for him; a team patch possibly worn by Thurman when he played for the Seran Agency, a scorebook from the same time period and a signed baseball by Thurman and Hall of Fame pitcher Bob Feller— a coach for an opponent the Seran Agency beat at the Stan Musial World Series in Battle Creek, Michigan.

I'd always wanted to own a signed Thurman Munson baseball, and on those few occasions when I felt ready to go ahead with buying one, there was something stopping me, that inner-voice I'd so relied upon at such times telling me the time wasn't right. I had no idea where any Munson ball may have been signed at, be it the Yankee Stadium dugout or someplace else, and I wanted to visualize that moment, not pretend to know. And while I longed for a signed baseball by Thurman Munson, I never felt a real connection and let it go.

It was a few weeks later on Easter Sunday of 2019 when I got a call from Gary. He was in his car with his wife Maureen and I was on my way to church, preparing to sing with the church choir.

We had our usual small talk when Gary said, "Tom, the day I told you about receiving those amazing gifts from Doug Miller, I told my wife about them. And before I could even get out the words, she said, "You are giving that ball to Tom, right? I said to her, "You know me too well."

There was a slight pause in our conversation when Gary said, "Yes, Tom. I'm giving you the ball. And I'm giving the patch to Adrienne. You two are the biggest Thurman Munson fans I know. You deserve this more than I do."

As I contemplated his words, I was literally speechless. It's hard to put into words I was so grateful and shocked. With tears in my eyes and that veil of humility and gratitude overtaking me, we decided it best to meet in person for the exchange, and what better place than at the entrance to the Hall of Fame three months to the day on induction weekend.

We'd kept busy in those three months, adding signatures to our petition and gaining support at Yankee Stadium where we paraded around with our *Munson for the Hall of Fame* banner on Old Timers' Day. We'd completed our proposals and Rene and Larry had done their best to get them into the voters hands. But when the day finally came for us to meet in Cooperstown, I couldn't help but think about the ball.

I have never been a big collector of baseball memorabilia or autographs over the years, but I will say I'm a picky one. My pride and joy, of course is my copy of, *Thurman Munson's Decade of Excellence* Chris Hahn and I wrote together, and the signatures I've acquired on it over the years from Roy White, Bucky Dent, Lou Piniella, Reggie Jackson, "Goose" Gossage and Ron Guidry— teammates of Thurman during the championship seasons 1977-78. I've had some chances for other Yankees I've admired to sign my copy, but if they weren't on either of those rosters for those two years— I passed.

It was a beautiful day in Cooperstown. Suzette and I and an entourage of family members walked Main Street towards the Hall of Fame as I thought about what was about to happen. I'd played in a similar league Thurman played on when he signed that ball. Our goal was the same— to make it to Battle Creek and play for the Stan Musial World Series championship. But our heartbreaking loss took away that dream of ours and my dream to play on the same field Thurman played on. Knowing that the ball I was about to lay eyes on for the first time, to lay hands for the first time, was everything to me right then.

We approached the Hall and spotted Gary with Rene LeRoux at its entrance. There was a lot of people walking around as I gathered my thoughts— thoughts I'd been having for those entire three months. Gary said a few words then introduced Rene. (The following is from that actual transcript).

Rene stood next to Gary, holding the ball encased in a hard plastic holder. Fans begin stopping to see what was happening and Rene said, "I'm

Rene LeRoux, and we're tying very hard to get Thurman Munson— the Yankee great... their captain— here into Cooperstown, his last resting place in a place that he deserves to be in. I'm joined by Gary Kaschak and Tom Tunison, members of the Munson Hall of Fame Committee. We have a very special presentation to make today... a very special day... and I'll give this ball to Gary so he can present it to Tom."

Gary spoke about our committee, the assignments Rene had given each of us and how he'd acquired the baseball. He said, "I had the privilege in talking with six people who so loved Thurman Munson like a brother. One in particular was Doug Miller who sent me some Munson treasures he'd had for over 50 years just out of the kindness of his heart. A Thurman Munson scorebook and team patch when he played for Seran Agency when he was 16 and this baseball signed by Thurman and Bob Feller. When Doug sent these to me I reminded him there was some value on that ball and it mattered not to him, he said I was the right one to receive that ball. Gary mentioned the talk we'd had on Easter Sunday, the stories told earlier on this chapter and the story of the ball.

As he continued speaking, I had no idea that Doug Miller was listening in, that Gary had his cell-phone on and Doug had heard every word spoken. When Gary said, "I'm gonna let Doug Miller -on the phone- to present the ball to Tom because its truly coming from him and not from me."

Gary raised the speaker volume on his cell-phone as high as it could go, and Doug Miller said, "Hi Tom, everything Gary was saying there was true. He was 16 going on 17 and the thing my dad was amazed was he talked about Thurman Munson being a middle infielder. That's an authentic baseball with Bob Feller and Thurman Munson from the first game of the state tournament in 1966 when Feller managed the opposing team. When then game was over and we won 5-4, Thurman asked Bob if he would autograph the baseball and when he did Thurman Munson autographed the same ball... I think this is great... I think what you're doing is great." I stood next to Gary and Rene, so many emotions grabbing me at once. I looked at my beautiful wife, the surrounding blue sky and the dozens of people who'd stopped out of curiosity. I said, "Doug, I really don't know what to say. Its unbelievable, such a great story and this incredible gift that you've given me it's just amazing... he's a legend and a great player and I'm blown away as you can imagine. That *Thurman Munson* signed that ball all those years ago and all these years later for it to end up in the hands of a guy like me. I tell you what... his family knows... Diana... and the kids.... they know... my wife knows... God bless her. My family knows, my friends here all know... our Hall of Fame Committee of Rene and Gary and Larry and Adrienne... they know how much this means to me... He was legend... a legendary catcher... he was a great catcher... he was a great teammate... he gave everything he had to the game of baseball.. and he was even a better man in person because he gave everything he had to his family. And now we're asking the family of baseball and the Cooperstown family... we're just asking them to do the right thing for Thurman Munson and his family. Forty years is long enough. It's a great institution and we're asking them to put their arms around him and his family and bring him home... bring him home here to Cooperstown. Thank you so much, Doug. I'm blown away. Thurman Munson for the Hall of Fame! Doug... thank you my friend, and I can't wait to meet you."

Gary shook my hand, and I said, "I don't deserve this ball, but for some reason I'm holding this ball right now. I'm a very happy man, very grateful, but the key here is *Thurman Munson for the Hall of Fame.*"

Chapter 21
New York State of Mind

"The normally bustling main Hall was utterly quiet and peaceful, its busts and plaques of Hall of Fame players surrounding us, almost as if they knew what was about to happen, an energy I could really sense."

I'd been running on mostly adrenaline for an entire year. Burning the midnight oil researching other contemporary great catcher's was necessary in building an even stronger case for Thurman. Statistical comparisons to Carlton Fisk and Johnny Bench was the logical place to start, then later adding Ted Simmons to the mix became a grueling marathon of late nights and little sleep.

But there were no limits to a labor of love that had consumed me. In the final push to get Thurman Munson noticed— to get him onto the ballot—was what mattered most. I'd have to push through the many sleep-deprived nights I knew I'd be facing, the many sleepless nights of tossing and turning, the anxiousness to start my day despite how tired I might be. And the fact that my research inside the numbers was highly favorable to Thurman's cause, well, I couldn't wait for the world to know what I'd uncovered.

I ran between New York and New Jersey taping segments we ended up posting on you-tube and other platforms with 87 Media company. I ran between my home in Bath and the New York State Baseball Hall of Fame in Troy to tape other segments, then returned home that night exhausted from the 400 mile round trip. And I taped a segment at the foot of Yankee Stadium earlier that year. But the drive home on each occasion was time to focus on the prize and the prize alone, and for that to happen, I new I'd need to go the distance.

It was just a few months later in November when Rene invited the members of the Munson Hall of Fame Committee to his annual induction ceremonies/dinner at his New York State Baseball Hall of Fame in Troy, New York. With an all-star studded cast of ex-Yankees being inducted or speaking on behalf of others, it promised to be another memorable event in a year that was full of them.

I'd only heard about the NYSBHOF after Rene took charge of our committee. To say I was intrigued and drawn to it like a moth to the flame would be putting it mildly. It certainly wasn't your usual Hall of Fame where players or coaches were inducted mostly from the merits of on-field accomplishments. There was a special balance to it, one that recognized achievement from a variety of position, so thought-provoking and utterly limitless in its reach. *A look inside the numbers.* But on this night... this one very special night... Thurman Munson was going in.

There was a sellout crowd at the ballroom that night, 491 people gathered to listen to and pay tribute to the likes of Bob Costas, Rich Aurilia, Ron Darling, Bill Madden, Howie Rose and Yankees Gene Monahan, Ron Guidry, Ray Negron, Bobby Murcer and Thurman Munson.

I took a moment to scan the room once we were seated and Rene started speaking. With my entire family seated with me at a table near the center of the room, I watched Diana Munson and Bobby Murcer's widow, Kay, just a few tables away from ours, talking to each other like old friends. I watched Ron Guidry talking with Goose Gossage who'd been invited to speak about Thurman, and as I tried to make some sense of where I was and how I'd reached this point, I couldn't help but think about the Bobby Murcer Tribute game or meeting Ron Guidry at Batavia Downs and how each event had been part of my journey to this place. And as I studied the faces of each member of my family seated with me, I nodded and smiled to myself.

There are some special moments in life that take you by surprise and there were several that night. When Rene began his introductory speech, he asked each of the Munson Committee members to stand and be recognized. I pulled my chair out and stood proudly like a soldier in front of my family, each of them smiling proudly. And when I looked to my right and saw Adrienne, Larry and Gary standing together, it was a moment frozen in time.

The speeches, well, they were memorable ones. That Gene Monahan— the Yankees long time trainer— would be inducted into a baseball Hall of Fame, and that Ray Negron— the long time Yankee batboy— were going in together along with Guidry, Murcer and Munson told me a lot about LeRoux. That Rene had talked to me about being a board advisor a few months earlier and offered it to me earlier in the evening was a mute point. I'd proudly accepted that offer long before the speeches began. But when Negron brought the house down with a speech for the ages, and Gossage stole the show going overtime in his love for Thurman, I knew I'd made the right call.

But the surprises weren't quite over with. That I'd been recognized along with my fellow committee members and accepted a position on Rene's board of directors made me feel as happy and humble as a man could feel. My plate of joy was full to the brim, but when Diana Munson took the stage and mentioned my name for the efforts she'd known I'd been making, I was absolutely floored by that and still am today.

It would be just two years later when an endorsement and recommendation for the Hall of Fame I'd made for John Morris would be accepted, and another regarding Mickey Watts Stapleton—my good friend and longtime battery mate Craig Stapleton's mother—would become reality, and that Craig would represent his entire family in speaking about her, choking back tears of joy for the *very first* woman player inductee into our Hall of Fame. To be in a position that could change lives like that may have been life-changing for some, impacting me directly, the biggest prize of all remained to be Thurman Munson for Cooperstown.

It was quite an evening when the speeches were over and the crowds trickled down. I sat with Gary, Larry, Marc Gambino, Billy Carr and Mario Rivera, Jr. in the hotel lobby— friends we'd made from the Munson fan pages— talking about the speeches and the whole Munson journey. And while we may have been the last ones to return to our rooms, their was yet another day to look forward to.

There was great irony in the fact that the Hall of Fame ballot would be announced the following day, another in a string of uncanny coincidences Gary and I had noticed for some time now. That our TV appearance in Binghamton *coincided* with the Rumble Ponies taping segments for their mural on the same day was hard to believe, but two more main events happening on back-to-back days was more than peculiar. And because of Troy's proximity to Cooperstown, we decided to travel there the following day for the ballot announcement where we'd stand together inside the Hall waiting for the announcement.

This would be my second trip to Cooperstown in less than six months, and I was looking forward to it as if I'd never been there before. There's just something magical about Cooperstown. The quaintness of Main Street and its pace of life takes you back in time to the Americana of my grandparents that's hard to find anymore. There's an atmosphere when you walk the street that's hard to define. It gets inside you and stimulates you, it opens your mind and soul, it slows you down to the intended pace around you, and it protects you, sealing off the world around you magically as you take it all in, escaping your worries and your problems, if only for a day. You see it on the faces of those around you, passing you on the street, and you wonder if they're thinking the same of you. Perhaps they'd been inside the Museum already, perhaps they're on their way. Either way, Main Street needs to be navigated to get there.

It's a Yellow Brick Road journey of inexplicable design, its small shops and memorabilia stores, its restaurants and on-street parking setting the tone. Set back no more than a few hundred feet from the street stands Doubleday Field, where greats like Mickey Mantle, Ted Williams and Hank Aaron showcased their talents. You walk the street and you know who'd been there before. When you were much younger, players bigger than life held your fascination, men you only read about or listened to on the radio or watched on TV. And as you pause to relive such memories, you are held in awe and veiled in humility because you know very well that you're standing where they once stood.

The drive there was therapeutic. Country roads that wind around to more country roads with no traffic to speak of.. Cars replaced by tractors and buggies, people replaced by livestock. And as country roads led to woods and lakes, you're suddenly there.

But this is off-season Cooperstown. No traffic, no long lines to get into the Hall of Fame, a ghost town of sorts. *The memories are still there.*

I parked behind Gary and we walked the half mile of Main Street towards the Hall, a nice, even pace with no need for speed. When we reached the grand structure and stood below its handful of concrete stairs, I studied its architecture and design, its brick facade and size not competing at all with the intimacy of Main Street, not intimidating or looking out of place. I nodded, took the stairs and opened the glass door and entered Oz, thinking of Thurman Munson.

We had the place to ourselves as we explored its rooms and hallways, its history and unpretentious magnificence. We took a lunch break and walked along Main Street again, then headed back to the Hall for the announcement.

We stood there alone for a while, then two of our buddies—Marc Gambino and Mario Rivera, Jr— surprised us. They'd found out we'd be there for the announcement and wanted to be with us when it was made. There was just a few minutes before the announcement, so we huddled together right there in the middle of the Hall.

It was as quiet as a church and I found great irony in that. The normally bustling main hall was utterly silent and peaceful, its busts and plaques of Hall of Fame players surrounding us, almost as if they knew what was about to happen, an energy I could really sense. To this point it had been one of the most perfect weekends of my life and I knew in my gut Thurman's name would be called. I held my cell-phone in my hand, waiting for my son, Dan to relay the news to us, closed my eyes and prayed that I was right.

There was an immense joy when Thurman's name *was called*. A victory like no other. The four of us embraced and made some phone calls, then headed to the closest restaurant to celebrate. We raised our glasses and raised them again, celebrating this latest victory.

Chapter 22
Hall Of Fame Announcement: Binghamton

"I bowed my head and looked at home plate. And as I thought about the path we'd just cleared for Thurman, I thought about my path, my journey and wondered if I'd finally gone the distance."

Making plans for the Hall of Fame announcement was a big deal that I'd discussed with Gary since the day the ballot was announced. Since our trip to Binghamton and then on to Cooperstown, *setting* had been a big deal to us. For all we'd done together and to represent Thurman properly, it didn't seem right to be apart. Wherever we'd end up it was imperative to be somewhere special, a place where we could feel the strength and the energy of Thurman Munson.

When we first met in Binghamton we wore our Sunday best on our TV interview and to my way of thinking it could be no other way. To that point we'd done all our work from afar with phone calls, texts and emails, but under the lights of the stage and in front of an audience we needed to represent Thurman Munson and the Thurman Munson family with the respect they deserved.

The logical choice to meet would be Canton, Ohio. There likely was no better place on earth where Thurman's energy could yet exist, that residual, invisible etherial veil of power that I so believe in. Holding a vigil at a number of places in Canton was discussed, but as hopeful as we were regarding the final vote, and knowing there was a chance for a big letdown, emotions would be running high one way or the other, and Diana and her children needed to have that moment to themselves.

We considered Cooperstown, but we'd been there when the ballot was announced and Thurman had no connection at all to it. I hadn't thought about it that way before, and it brought a tear to me eye when I did. *Travesty*, I thought.

We considered Yankee Stadium, but knew we couldn't get close enough to its entrance. We considered Dunn Field in Elmira where both Thurman and I played ball there at separate times, and because of that would always be a special place for me, a place where I felt connected to Thurman. But as we talked about significance of location and what it meant to us, we landed on Binghamton as the place we'd like to meet at again.

As Thurman's first stop on his pro tour, Binghamton certainly held a great deal of significance in his life. That I'd interviewed together with Gary on Binghamton TV, had our tapings done at the Rumble Ponies home park, met some great baseball people along the way and was Gary's native town, Binghamton was where we wanted to be most.

The old Johnson Field where Thurman played in 1968 had been long torn down, a victim of eminent domain and the long arm of progress, so that was out of the question. We discussed setting up camp at the site of where Johnson Field once stood, but a highway had taken its place. And as we checked off boxes of where we should go, the only logical place was back to NYSEG Stadium, home of the Rumble Ponies.

We knew it was going to be a long shot asking for access to the stadium, but we wanted badly to be inside, even on the field prior to or when the announcement was made. And while we knew that Thurman never set foot on its field or in its locker room, his memory was still there in other ways. The Binghamton mural with his image prominently placed and the words we'd spoken about him was proof enough for me.

When Gary approached Director of Community Relations Eddie Saunders to plead our case, there was no hesitation whatsoever. When Saunders reached out to team general manager John Bayne to discuss our request, there was no red-tape or hoops to jump through, they'd open the stadium for us the night of the announcement.

I'm not sure how many teams would have done that for us or anyone else for that matter, but it can't be many. To open an entire stadium in the dead of winter with no special paperwork to sign or even charging a fee was unfathomable. Everything Gary told me about Binghamton was true. Down the line from Kara Conrad, Steve Popolski, Jim Maggiore, Roger Neel, John Taylor, Eddie Saunders and John Bayne, there was a pulse that beat as one, refreshing attitudes of understanding and of doing the right thing for others. Gary was lucky to have been brought up here. *My kind of people.*

While we were fortunate to have persuaded Eddie to allow us access to the stadium, I wasn't feeling particularly positive about Thurman's chances and hadn't for a while. National writers and announcers had a lot to say about the ballot and those who were on it, but Thurman's name rarely came up with any positive spin to it. Instead, they cited his "lack of everything." Not enough hits or RBI, not enough home runs, not enough this or that. It was the same old routine with no thought given to the numbers I'd tried sharing with the world. The frustration was concerning. Whatever it was they had to say about Thurman, they sure didn't know him like I did, and that was the problem.

I drove to Binghamton the night of the announcement with Suzette, hoping that some national broadcaster had come to his senses. But as I turned on the radio and listened to the chatter and rhetoric from the so called "experts" on what was likely going to happen in a few hours, I turned the radio off.

There'd been a giant snowstorm the day before leaving a foot of snow on the ground all the way from our part of the state and west into Binghamton, leaving us concerned that Eddie would need to call the whole thing off, leaving us with nowhere to go. But we'd gotten the sense he had bought into our efforts, that he was pulling for Thurman us as much as we were. And despite a foot of snow that nearly closed off some streets, and in the true spirit of kindness, concern and effort, Eddie opened the stadium for us and led us into the home locker room.

He'd fashioned some makeshift signs indicating where people should go when they arrived. We'd shared on the Munson Fan Page where we'd be for the announcement, making sure any Munson fans living in the area had a chance to join us. Gary's childhood friend John Taylor and a few others were there, and our Munson friends— Marc Gambino, who'd been with us in Cooperstown when the ballot was announced— and Lou Rivera, who'd started a Munson blog on Twitter — drove hundreds of miles from out of town to join us. We'd had conversations with them about being together for the announcement, to be together for something historic, and despite the distance and the weather, they made the trip.

Saunders had set up a TV set in the locker room and had set it to the *Baseball Channel* when we arrived. I took a cursory glance and listened half-heartedly to what the panel of experts had to say, but had heard enough already. The die had been cast. At that point Gary asked Eddie if we could have access to the field and without hesitation, Eddie clicked on the field lights and the four of us- myself, Gary, Marc and Lou— entered the dugout and looked onto the field.

There was something surreal looking upon a baseball field blanketed in a foot of snow. There was no wind or even a sound around the ballpark, its empty seats covered in white, its light towers flickering under an initial surge of power, shedding light across the diamond. *Beautiful.* We decided to clear off home plate, making a path of some sort to honor Thurman, *to give him a place to be.*

Despite the depth of the snow we trudged onto the field, looking for a patch of ground with a good background for taking photos. We walked around the field for a while then settled on a patch of ground in shallow center field just behind the infield. It seemed to be a good place to take photos. The middle of the field offered an openness that had no borders to its side and the center field wall added that baseball field dimension I was looking for. We took turns standing in the outfield as photos were taken from the mound, each of us standing in the exact same spot. We took a few group shots then headed towards home plate.

We'd cleared enough room for the four of us to stand inside both batters boxes, facing home plate. And while there'd been no discussion whatsoever regarding saying a prayer or giving thanks, we circled around it, wrapped our arms around each other and said a prayer.

Impromptu prayer circles can be powerful, and this one certainly was. Four friends, all from different parts of the country, gathered together, united for a cause. I had no idea what any of their beliefs were, if they'd been church-going, atheists or non-believers. And none of that mattered. In that moment I knew *all of us* were believers and that the four silent prayers we'd sent off had similar messages.

I bowed my head, looked at home plate and as I thought about the path we'd just cleared for Thurman, I thought about my path, my *journey* and wondered if I'd finally gone the distance and asked Thurman *to send me a sign.*

"It's time," said Eddie. "The announcement is in 10 minutes."

When we returned to the locker room, I hugged Suzette gently, holding her for the comfort she always provided. And when 10 minutes went down to five, Gary asked me to say a few words. I paused for a moment, just standing there. There was a million independent thoughts firing through my mind right then, a million thoughts going back to my childhood. I cleared my throat and said, (actual transcript).

"Well, my heart's beating pretty good... It really is. And it's just awesome to see all these die-hard Thurman Munson fans here. There's so many that wish they can be here, but for those of us that are here, it's a big night for the Munson Family. God bless them... we want this so bad for them. They deserve this... Thurman deserves this... and baseball history deserves this... this man deserves his place in the Hall of Fame in Cooperstown.

We're all Thurman fans and we're all baseball fans and Thurman... this is your day. Please. Let it be his day for the family, Diana and the kids, today is the day, December 8th, 2019. Thurman Munson for the Hall of Fame.

The next few moments were agonizing as the list of names being announced grew shorter. I kept repeating to myself, *Thurman Munson... Thurman Munson... Thurman Munson...* but his name wasn't called. Just like that it was over.

There wasn't much solace I could be given at that moment. Moral victories have never given me much satisfaction, and neither would this one. Getting as far as we had to only fall short wasn't bittersweet at all. It was all bitter.

Sure, we'd succeeded to get Thurman on the ballot, his many decades spent lost inside the politics of baseball pulled out from a dormancy that took root his first year of eligibility and festered into near oblivion. There certainly was a great deal of satisfaction helping getting him noticed again, to have his name become relevant again. In many ways we wouldn't be going back to square one, but in some ways we were. There'd be other players who'd be eligible for induction, others from Thurman's era to be bandied about. There'd be no guarantee that Thurman would "move up" or remain on the next ballot. Players like Dick Allen fell one vote short *twice* then had his voting numbers plummet, a travesty of baseball justice that needs to be fixed.

But despite the disappointment we all felt when Thurman's name wasn't called, the five of us headed to The Little Venice restaurant to celebrate. Of course it wasn't the celebration we wanted, the one we'd expected. We sat at the bar and toasted the effort, toasted each other, Thurman, Diana and her children. To life and friends. As we shared what that year had brought to us, we shared the photos we'd taken on the snowy field.

It didn't take long to notice the individual photos we'd taken of each other standing in center field and for something peculiar standing out. It was the light shining down on me as I folded my hands in prayer.

I'll never be able to explain that beam of light shining down on me from the light towers, or be able to explain why it hadn't on the others. I'm sure there's some logical explanation regarding angle, position, lighting, whatever, that can be given by an expert in the field. All I know is that it happened. That I'd silently asked Thurman to provide me a sign during our prayer circle at home plate and to see this now was an answer to my prayer. Whatever it was, I know what I believe.

When I first started believing that *going the distance* exclusively meant Thurman for the Hall of Fame, that mindset changed somewhat along the way. I realized that *the going* was hardly complete, that I was *going* to visit Canton one day, that I was *going* to place a copy of the Thurman poem I wrote gently at his gravesite and that I was *going* to build my baseball academy.

I realized that the *distance* meant more than just miles or time or any other unit of measurement you can think of, and certainly didn't mean it was final, its concept separated only by the imagination and the will to continue.

There was a light shining down on me that night in Binghamton, but it had always been there. What Thurman Munson has given me in my life is as real as that inexplicable beam cast from that stadium light. And no matter how long it may take to see all this through, I will continue to *go the distance* for him.

Final Thoughts

I knew when we first started "Go the Distance" it was meant to shine the light on the great career of and the man Thurman Munson. Thankfully now that we have finally reached this moment that purpose and focus still remains. My admiration for Thurman as a player and as a person has only grown throughout this journey as I have poured over his statistics for more hours than I can remember.

It has been a joy to discover so many things about his career that I didn't know about. To search throughout the history of baseball catchers and to see how he stands out amongst them in so many ways.

The journey of "Going the Distance " has only helped to strengthen my stance for Thurman.

He truly is one of the greatest catchers in the history of baseball and he deserves to be enshrined in Cooperstown in The National Baseball Hall of Fame. His family deserves to see this honor take place. They are wonderful people and I am extremely happy to have met them and to call them friends. I cannot say enough about the beautiful Diana Munson and the time and care that she gives to Thurman's fans...it's very, very special.

What I didn't know when we started this book was the way it would make me look back on and reflect on my life in such a profound way. As a person you realize where you are at in your life, you know what you've been through to get to this point but without really taking the time to focus and reflect on the important people and moments of your life you are missing out.

This time of reflection has given me great pause to realize just what it took for my family to help get me through the difficult times of my childhood. The care that my siblings and my parents gave me while I couldn't walk... I can't repay. I love them very much and I need them to know that. My doctors, Dr. Caso and Dr. Trinkle... I am forever indebted to them for curing me and for giving me my life back.

My friends from my childhood and all of the fun we had while playing ball, riding bikes, going to the beach and just being kids...it was incredible.

The most important and biggest thing this experience has given me is that it has made me focus on those moments when God carried me through the sand. When I was weak and at my lowest points of my young life he never abandoned me, and when I paid attention and loved him back... he answered my prayers in the affirmative.

All glory to God.

That day at the ocean when it was freezing cold in the dead of winter and I was all alone staring at that great big sea I had a decision to make. I wasn't thinking very good thoughts, and I was very lonely, angry and yes... very scared.

But God nudged me, grabbed hold of me and made me feel very, very small right at a critical moment. And in doing so he shrunk my problems that so consumed my soul down to nothing. He made me see right then and there that this big old world wasn't just about me and my problems. It's about all if us... every life matters.

And right then and there I knew I was going to make it. I knew I had work to do to get my life back on track... I knew it wouldn't be easy but I was going to make it... I was going to "Go the Distance ".

While attending church one Sunday recently at the Grace Bible Baptist church, seated close by my good friend Michael Hall, his son, Pastor Garrett Hall was preaching to us about how much God loves us. During this particular sermon he wanted us to really pay attention. Not just to him. More importantly he wanted us to pay attention to God. He explained to us that if we're not hearing from God lately that there's probably a good reason. It's probably because we're not paying attention to God. If you want to hear from God...pay attention, listen and he will show you how much he loves you... and great things will happen in your life.

Thank you Gary for giving me this gift.
Your friend,
Tom

About the Authors

Tom Tunison

Tom Tunison is a baseball historian/statistician and member of the *Thurman Munson Hall Of Fame Committee* where he served in both capacities. As a first year member of the New York State Baseball Hall of Fame Board of Directors, his research and subsequent nominations of John Morris, Billy Blitzer and Mickey Watts Stapleton led to their inductions, with Watts Stapleton becoming the first woman inductee into its Hall of Fame. He's coached youth baseball for a quarter century and co-authored (with Christopher Hahn) *Thurman Munson's Decade of Unmatched Excellence.*

Gary Kaschak

Gary Kaschak has served as sports writer and/or columnist for The *Vestal News* (upper New York State), The *Green Bay Press Gazette* (Wisconsin) and *The Burlington County Times* (New Jersey). He served the *Montrose Independent* (Pennsylvania) as its Sports Editor. He was Statistician for the 1981 Washington Federals (a team in the now-defunct United States Football League); and he's served as sports reporter for WKOP radio, out of Binghamton, New York. He's covered Major League Baseball Hall of Fame induction ceremonies for the *Cooperstown Crier* and the *Oneonta Daily Star.* He's served as head-writer for two baseball committees; *The Dummy Hoy Hall of Fame Committee* and *The Thurman Munson Hall of Fame Committee* and is Editor for The New York State Baseball Hall of Fame's, *Extra Innings* He's written five books: *Hands That Break... Hands That Heal,* and, *The Hole To China,* both well-received teen sports/inspirational novels, and, *Lifestone,* a murder mystery set during America's Civil War. *My Name Was Mickey Mantle,* and, *Coming Home. My Amazin' life as a New York Met* (The Cleon Jones story).

Note from the Author

Word-of-mouth is crucial for any author to succeed. If you enjoyed *Go the Distance*, please leave a review online—anywhere you are able. Even if it's just a sentence or two. It would make all the difference and would be very much appreciated.

Thanks!
Tom Tunison

We hope you enjoyed reading this title from:

www.blackrosewriting.com

Subscribe to our mailing list – *The Rosevine* – and receive **FREE** books, daily deals, and stay current with news about upcoming releases and our hottest authors.
Scan the QR code below to sign up.

Already a subscriber? Please accept a sincere thank you for being a fan of Black Rose Writing authors.

View other Black Rose Writing titles at www.blackrosewriting.com/books and use promo code **PRINT** to receive a **20% discount** when purchasing.

www.ingramcontent.com/pod-product-compliance
Lightning Source LLC
Chambersburg PA
CBHW072006070526
44583CB00015B/1359